teach®
yourself

AutoCAD 2004

mac bride

teach®
yourself

AutoCAD 2004
mac bride

For UK order enquiries: please contact Bookpoint Ltd, 130 Milton Park, Abingdon, Oxon OX14 4SB. Telephone: +44 (0) 1235 827720. Fax: +44 (0) 1235 400454. Lines are open 09.00–18.00, Monday to Saturday, with a 24-hour message answering service. Details about our titles and how to order are available at www.teachyourself.co.uk

For USA order enquiries: please contact McGraw-Hill Customer Services, PO Box 545, Blacklick, OH 43004-0545, USA. Telephone: 1-800-722-4726. Fax: 1-614-755-5645.

For Canada order enquiries: please contact McGraw-Hill Ryerson Ltd, 300 Water St, Whitby, Ontario L1N 9B6, Canada. Telephone: 905 430 5000. Fax: 905 430 5020.

Long renowned as the authoritative source for self-guided learning – with more than 40 million copies sold worldwide – the **teach yourself** series includes over 300 titles in the fields of languages, crafts, hobbies, business, computing and education.

British Library Cataloguing in Publication Data: a catalogue record for this title is available from the British Library.

Library of Congress Catalog Card Number: on file.

First published in UK 2004 by Hodder Education, 338 Euston Road, London, NW1 3BH.

First published in US 2004 by Contemporary Books, a Division of the McGraw-Hill Companies, 1 Prudential Plaza, 130 East Randolph Street, Chicago, IL 60601 USA.

This edition published 2004

The **teach yourself** name is a registered trade mark of Hodder Headline.

Computer hardware and software brand names mentioned in this book are protected by their respective trademarks and are acknowledged.

Copyright © 2004 Mac Bride

Typeset by MacDesign, Southampton

Printed in Great Britain for Hodder Education, a division of Hodder Headline, 338 Euston Road, London NW1 3BH, by Cox & Wyman Ltd, Reading, Berkshire.

Hodder Headline's policy is to use papers that are natural, renewable and recyclable products and made from wood grown in sustainable forests. The logging and manufacturing processes are expected to conform to the environmental regulations of the country of origin.

Impression number   10 9 8 7 6 5 4

Year   2010 2009 2008 2007 2006 2005

contents

	preface	ix
01	**introducing AutoCAD**	**1**
	starting AutoCAD	2
	the AutoCAD window	2
	the toolbars	2
	the mouse in AutoCAD	5
	model space and paper space	7
	starting a drawing	8
	zoom	11
	drawing with the mouse	12
	snap	13
	object snap	14
	specifying coordinates	16
	the Line tool	17
	saving and closing files	19
	opening files	21
	exercises	23
02	**the drawing tools**	**25**
	the Draw menu and the toolbar	26
	rectangles	26
	circles	30
	construction lines	31
	polygons	32

	arcs	33
	splines	35
	ellipses	36
	ellipse arcs	37
	points	37
	polylines	38
	selecting and editing objects	42
	exercises	44
03	**modifying objects**	**47**
	the modify toolbar	48
	erase	48
	copy	49
	mirror	50
	offset	52
	array	52
	move	55
	rotate	55
	scale	56
	stretch	57
	trim and extend	58
	break	59
	chamfer	61
	fillet	62
	explode	63
	exercises	64
04	**properties**	**66**
	the Properties toolbar	67
	lineweight	67
	linetype	69
	line colour	71
	the Properties palette	73
	exercises	77
05	**fills and hatches**	**79**
	hatching	80

	gradient fills	85
	exercises	87
06	**text and dimensions**	**89**
	text on drawings	90
	single line text	90
	multiline text	92
	adding dimensions	93
	leaders	100
	dimension style	102
	exercises	107
07	**layers**	**109**
	what are layers?	110
	creating layers	113
	objects and layers	115
	exercises	116
08	**blocks and the designcenter**	**117**
	blocks	118
	the DesignCenter	123
	inserting a block	124
	DC Online	126
	exercises	128
09	**from sketch to plot**	**129**
	sketches	130
	orthographic projection	131
	model space and paper output	133
	setting up and drawing	136
	layouts	137
	viewports	140
	plotters and plotting	142
	exercises	146
10	**drawing in 3D**	**148**
	3D modes	149
	the Z coordinate	149
	3D polyline	152

viii

contents

	tips for drawing in 3D	153
	plotting 3D drawings	154
	exercises	156
11	**3D solids**	**157**
	defining solids	158
	combining solids	163
	the Shade options	167
	rendering	168
	exercises	173
	taking it further	**175**
	index	**177**

preface

AutoCAD is the world's leading Computer Aided Design (CAD) software, used by architects, engineers, draughtsmen and other professionals to create 2D or 3D drawings and models. It is a very powerful and sophisticated package, capable of handling the most complex constructions, but it is also well-designed and logical, and so not too hard to get started with.

The aim of this book is to introduce AutoCAD's key tools and techniques. It assumes that you have enough understanding of Windows to be able to start a program, save and open files, and use the Internet. A high level of Windows competence is not needed – and in fact, may not help. AutoCAD started life in the days before Windows, and some of its operations will not seem intuitive to people who have only ever used Windows software.

AutoCAD is a huge package, and this is a small book, so I have had to be very selective about what has gone in. I hope that you will find here the grounding that you need to get started and the confidence to go on and explore more of the potential of the system.

Mac Bride

2004

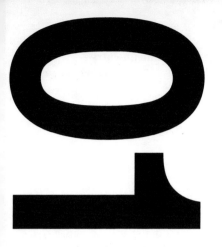

01

introducing AutoCAD

In this chapter you will learn:

- about the AutoCAD tools
- how to use the Command Line window
- how to specify coordinates
- about handling files in AutoCAD

Starting AutoCAD

AutoCAD can be started from its Start menu entry – you should find it in the Autodesk submenu – or from its Desktop shortcut.

AutoCAD 2004

When the AutoCAD window first opens, it should display a blank drawing ready for you to start work on a new project.

The AutoCAD window

The main areas and features of the AutoCAD window, are marked on the screenshot on page 3. Note these, in particular:

*   The **Drawing area** can display model space, or paper space layouts. Click on the tags at the bottom left to switch displays.

*   The **Command Line window** is used for entering coordinates. Commands can also be entered here, though it is often simpler to use the menus or toolbars.

*   The **Status bar** shows the coordinates of the cursor at the bottom left. In the centre and the right of the bar are toggles (on/off switches) for some key options. Note these two:

    If **Grid** is on, a rectangular pattern of dots is shown. These are normally 10 units apart.

    If **Snap** is on, the mouse jumps to the nearest snap point when you click.

The toolbars

AutoCAD has nearly 30 toolbars. These five toolbars are normally present, and are the most used.

*   The **Standard** toolbar contains the same filing, printing and copying tools that you will find in most Windows applications, plus tools to move and zoom around drawing, and ones to turn the Properties (page 73) and DesignCenter (page 123) windows on and off.

*   The **Properties** toolbar is used for setting the colour, weight and style of lines (see Chapter 4).

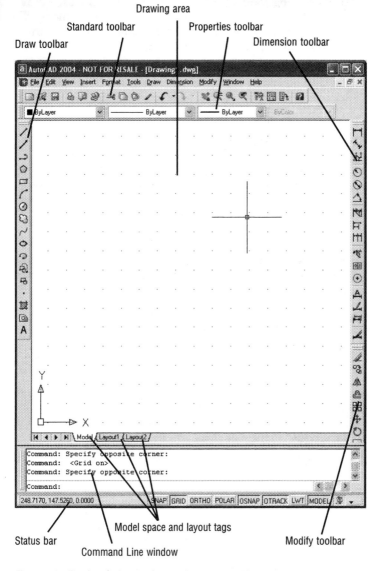

Drawing area

Standard toolbar

Properties toolbar

Draw toolbar

Dimension toolbar

Model space and layout tags

Status bar

Command Line window

Modify toolbar

Figure 1.1 The AutoCAD window when it first opens. Notice the tabs at the bottom of the working area. Drawings are created in model space (on the Model tab). The Layout tabs are used for plotting – leave these well alone until you are ready to start thinking about plotting. We will come to them in Chapter 9.

- The **Drawing** toolbar holds the most commonly used drawing tools. The full set can be found in the Draw menu. We will look at the Line tool later in this chapter, then return to the rest in Chapter 2.

- The **Modify** toolbar has tools for moving, rotating, mirroring and otherwise manipulating objects.

- The **Dimensions** toolbar has tools for marking dimensions on your drawings (see Chapter 6).

The toolbar layout is not fixed and can be easily changed to suit your current drawing. Toolbars can be turned on or off, and can be moved to new positions. A toolbar can be docked at the top or either side of the drawing area, or allowed to float anywhere on screen. Floating toolbars can have their tools in one long single line, or in a short multi-line block.

To turn toolbars on or off:

1 Right-click on any toolbar and the full list will appear. Those toolbars currently displayed will have ticks by their names.

2 Click on a toolbar name to toggle its display on or off.

To move a toolbar:

1 If the toolbar is docked against an edge, click on the double raised lines at the left/top. If it is floating, click on its title bar.

2 Drag the toolbar across the screen. An outline will appear to show its shape if placed at that point. If the toolbar is going to float, the outline will be drawn in a heavier line and will be a larger shape – as there will be a title bar.

3 Release the mouse button when you are in the right place. If the toolbar is being docked, it will automatically go to the left or the top of the docking area.

4 Toolbars can be moved within a docking area if required. Drag on the raised lines and release the outline when it is over the place where you want it to go.

To resize a floating toolbar:

1 Move the cursor over the side or bottom of the toolbar until it turns into a double-headed arrow.

2 Drag the arrow to change the shape of the toolbar.

Toolbar handle

The toolbar can be docked here...

... or left floating here

Drag to change the shape

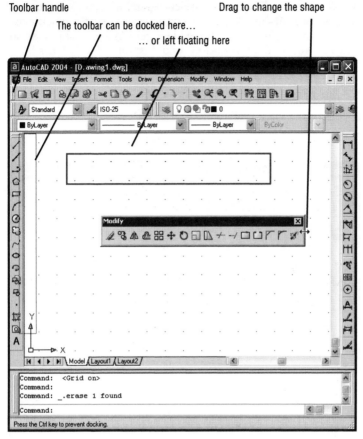

Figure 1.2 Toolbars can be moved and resized easily.

The mouse in AutoCAD

AutoCAD makes more use of the mouse than most Windows applications do.

The left button works as normal, but note the double-click:

- Click to select a tool or a drawn object, as usual.

- Click and drag to draw a line or shape, or to enclose and select a set of objects.

- Double-click on a drawn object to open its Properties panel.

A right button click on any object opens its context menu, as normal, but the button can be configured so that a quick click has the same effect as an [Enter] keypress. As [Enter] is used so much in AutoCAD, this option should be turned on. Here's how.

To customize the right button:

1 Open the **Tools** menu and select **Options...**

2 Go to the **User Preferences** tab.

3 In the top right section, click **Right-click Customization...**

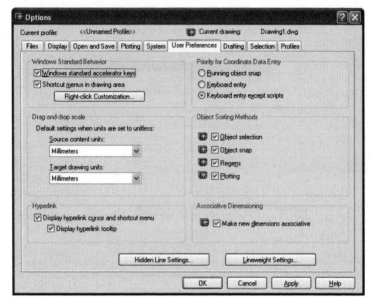

Figure 1.3 The User Preferences tab of the Options dialog box. Any of the settings can be changed at any time, but most are best left at their defaults at first. You might like to go to the Display tab where you can set the screen colour and other aspects of the display – I prefer a white background to the default black.

4 Tick the **Turn on time-sensitive right-click** checkbox.

5 The duration is set for 250 milliseconds. If you find you need a shorter or longer delay, come back to here and change it.

6 Click **Apply & Close**.

7 Back at the **Options** dialog box, click **OK** to close it.

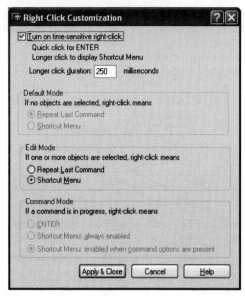

Figure 1.4 Customizing the right-click action.

The wheel mouse

If your mouse has a wheel between the buttons, this can be used to zoom and pan around your workspace.

♦ Roll the wheel forward to zoom in.

♦ Roll the wheel backwards to zoom out.

♦ Press the wheel in and drag the mouse to move the drawing within the workspace window.

Model space and paper space

In AutoCAD, drawings are created in '**model space**'. This can be of any size, measured in any units – metric or imperial, decimal or fractions. You could create a model space to fit inside a match-box, or to map the west coast line from London to Glasgow – and they would both feel much the same within AutoCAD. As the real world dimensions are scaled up or down as necessary to fit into model space, size is almost irrelevant – until you take the plans back to the real world!

You can move around in model space, viewing your drawing from any angle or distance. You can zoom in on details or pull back to see it all at once; you can look at it from a number of pre-set viewpoints or rotate the drawing in any of the three dimensions. Though model space is three-dimensional, the output can only be seen – on screen or on paper – in two dimensions. In practice, most AutoCAD drawings are two-dimensional, because this is what is needed. Drawings can be created in 3D, as you will see, but requires a little more work than drawing in 2D.

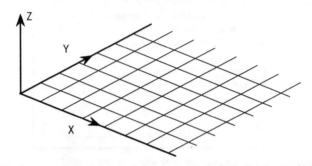

Figure 1.5 Model space is infinite, but you can define the width (X) and length (Y) of the drawing area. The height (Z) is not defined.

Outputs from AutoCAD are in '*paper space*'. Its size is set by the physical size of the sheets in your plotter or printer. The current screen image can be output to paper, or you can created *layouts*, which show part or all of the drawing, from a given viewpoint. Once a layout is defined, it is more or less fixed (adjustments are possible), but you can define as many as you need.

Starting a drawing

Before you can actually start work, you need to specify the units of measurement and the limits of the drawing area.

The drawing units can be:

Decimal	Millimetres
Engineering	Feet and inches (with decimals)
Architectural	Feet and inches (with fractions)
Fractional	Standard units and fractions
Scientific	Units, in exponential form

The default drawing limits are 420 by 297. These are suitable for use with A3 paper (420 × 297 mm), giving a simple translation of one drawing unit to one millimetre on paper. If you are using Imperial measurements, the default limits are 12 by 9. The limits can be anything, but if they are very different from the defaults, you may need to change the settings for the grid (page 13), the text (page 92) and the dimension text (page 104).

Drawings can be started from templates or wizards, or from scratch. There are templates for a range of paper sizes, and for a range of grids and information boxes – explore them at some point. The wizard is a slower way to set values that would otherwise be set through dialog boxes.

We will start from scratch.

1 Click the **New** button 🔲 or select **New** from the **File** menu.

2 At the **Create New Drawing** dialog box, click the **Start from scratch** button.

3 Select your **Default Settings – Imperial** or **Metric**.

4 Click **OK**.

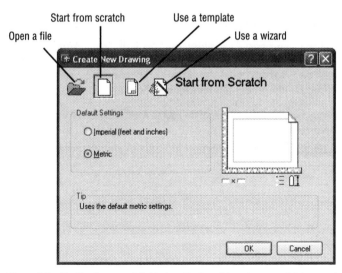

Figure 1.6 Starting from scratch. Explore the templates at some point to see what is available.

5 Open the **Format** menu and select **Units...**

6 At the **Drawing Units** dialog box, the **Length** and **Angle** units are normally *Decimal*. Change these if required.

7 **Precision** determines how accurately values are *displayed* (they are *stored* as accurately as possible). Set a level and click **OK**.

Figure 1.7 Setting the Drawing Units. Ignore the drag-and-drop scale until you start to use blocks (see Chapter 8).

8 Open the **Format** menu and select **Drawing Limits**.

9 In the Command Line window, you will be prompted for the coordinates of the lower left corner of the drawing area. The current values will be shown in angle brackets, e.g. <0.00,0.00>. Press [**Enter**] to accept these.

10 Enter the coordinates of the upper right corner. Give these in the form *width,length*.

```
Command: '_limits
Reset Model space limits:
Specify lower left corner or [ON/OFF] <0.00,0.00>: 0,0
Specify upper right corner <420.00,297.00>: 297,210
```

Tip!

When AutoCAD asks for input through the Command Line, it will sometimes offer default values or options. These will be shown in <angle brackets>. Press [Enter] or right-click to accept the defaults.

Zoom

You do not need a wheel mouse (page 7) to zoom, as there are two zoom tools on the Standard toolbar. **Zoom Window** expands a selected area to fill the screen; **Zoom Realtime** lets you move in and out flexibly.

To zoom in on a defined window:

1 Click on the **Zoom Window** button ![button].

2 Drag an outline over the area to be zoomed.

3 Click to fix the far corner.

To zoom in and out:

1 Click on the **Zoom Realtime** button ![button].

2 Drag the magnifying glass cursor up the screen to zoom in, or down to zoom out.

3 Press [**Escape**] to end zoom mode.

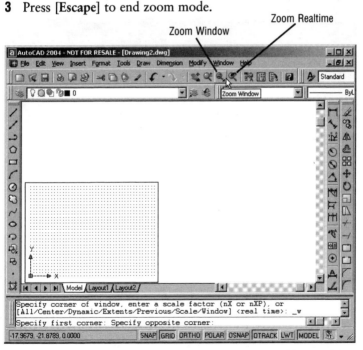

Figure 1.8 Using the Zoom window. With some drawing limits, the grid is so small that you need to zoom in before you can start work.

Drawing with the mouse

Objects are defined by specifying the positions of vertices or by a combination of positions and size or angles. They can be drawn with the mouse (or other pointing device) or the data can be typed into the Command Line, or you can use a mixture of both.

When you are drawing, clicking on the working area selects the current position – this is known as *picking*. Freehand drawing is best used for sketching, as it is virtually impossible to position the cursor accurately with any pointing device – look at the co-ordinates in the Status Bar and you will see that you can never get exactly on any point.

There are two ways to make your mouse work accurate:

+ **Snap** – when enabled, the mouse will jump to the nearest snap point when you click. Initially the snap points are the same as the visible grid points. Snap to grid is only useful, of course, if the object's vertices will fit on the grid.

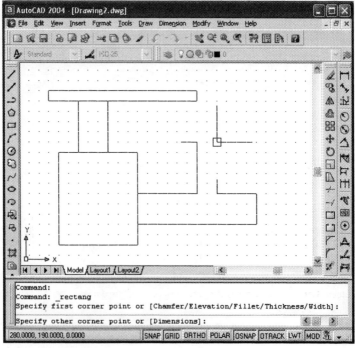

Figure 1.9 Snap makes mouse drawing more accurate.

- **Object Snap** – when enabled, the cursor will jump to the mid or endpoints of a existing line when you click near it.

There is also a **Polar tracking** mode. This shows the distance and angle of the cursor from the last point, but it does not force the cursor to lock onto a specific point as the Snap modes do.

Snap

We saw earlier that the grid, and the Snap mode can be toggled on and off by the Status Bar indicators. You do not need the grid on to use the Snap mode, and the snap and grid points do not have to coincide – though it helps if you snap to a visible grid.

The size of the visible grid and the spacing of the snap points can be adjusted through the Snap and Grid Settings.

1 Open the **Tools** menu and select **Drafting Settings...**

2 Go to the **Snap and Grid** tab.

Figure 1.10 The Snap and Grid spacing values do not need to be the same, and the X and Y values can differ.

3 Enter **Snap** and **Grid spacing** values to suit your drawing.

4 Click **OK**.

Object Snap

When Object Snap is active, you can click accurately onto the end, midpoint, centre or other significant point on an existing object. When the cursor is close to a snap point, a marker appears and the cursor will lock onto it when you click. There are a dozen types of snap points, which can be turned on independently. There is also an option to display the vector (distance and angle) of the cursor from the last drawing point.

The main options are controlled through the Drafting Settings.

1 Open the **Tools** menu and select **Drafting Settings...**

2 At the **Drafting Settings** dialog box, open the **Object Snap** tab.

3 Tick the **Object Snap On** checkbox to activate it.

4 Tick or clear the boxes to select the snap modes to activate.

5 Tick the **Object Snap Tracking On** checkbox if you want the distance and angle vector information.

6 Click **OK**.

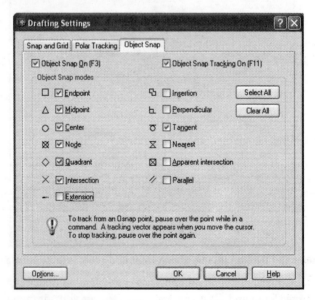

Figure 1.11   Activating Object Snap. If you are not going to use a snap mode, turn it off to reduce possible confusion.

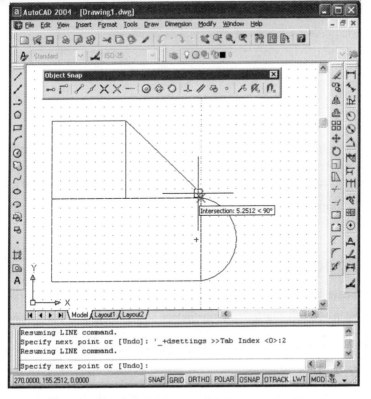

Figure 1.12 Using Object Snap. The green cross indicates a snap point at the intersection of the rectangle and the arc. The distance and angle data is displayed as tracking is turned on.

Single-use snap

If too many snap modes are active, a multiplicity of markers close together can make life difficult on a complex drawing. In other situations you may prefer to work with all snap modes normally turned off. In either case, there is a single-use snap mode that you can use from the Object Snap toolbar. This will turn on one snap mode while one point is defined.

To use single-use Object Snap:

1 If the Object Snap toolbar is not visible, right-click on any toolbar and tick **Object Snap** in the list of toolbars.

The Object Snap toolbar

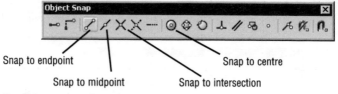

Snap to endpoint

Snap to midpoint

Snap to centre

Snap to intersection

2 Select your drawing tool.

3 When it is time to specify a coordinate, click on a snap mode button on the Object Snap toolbar.

4 Using the snap markers as guides, snap to and pick the point.

5 Repeat steps **4** and **5** for picking further points with the same drawing tool.

Specifying coordinates

There are three ways of giving coordinates in the Command Line.

◆ As simple **Cartesian** coordinates, in the form x,y. For example 200,150 specifies a point where x = 200 (i.e. 200 units to the right of 0,0), and y = 150 (i.e. 150 units up from 0,0).

◆ As **relative** coordinates, expressed as the distances from the last point, in the form '@x,y', e.g. @100,-25 specifies a point 100 units to the right and 25 units below the last point.

◆ As **polar** coordinates, giving the distance and angle from the last point, in the form '@distance<angle', e.g. @200<135 means 200 units and 135 degrees from the last point. Angles are normally measured anticlockwise, starting at 3 o'clock.

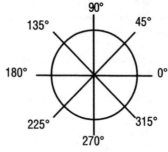

Figure 1.13 The default angle measurement in AutoCAD.

Clockwise angles

If you would prefer to use clockwise angle measurement, turn on the Clockwise option in the Drawing Units dialog box (see page 10).

```
Command: _rectang
Specify first corner point or [Chamfer/Elevation/Fillet/Thickness/Width]:
125,190
Specify other corner point or [Dimensions]: 308.5,149
```

Figure 1.14 The Command Window after defining a rectangle. Notice that when the command first started, the system asked for either the first corner point or for an option to be specified. Many AutoCAD commands offer a range of options.

```
Command: _rectang
Specify first corner point or [Chamfer/Elevation/Fillet/Thickness/Width]:
125,190
Specify other corner point or [Dimensions]: @183.5,-51
```

Figure 1.15 These command lines define the same rectangle as the ones above, but here the second corner is given in terms of distance from the first.

Feet and inches

If you are working with feet and inches and simply enter a number, AutoCAD will assume it is in inches. To enter a value in feet, type an apostrophe (') after the number.

The Line tool

Most drawing tools can only be used to draw a single object, and must be reselected to draw another. The Line tool is a little different. It can be used to draw a single line or a continuous sequence, with the endpoint of one being the startpoint of the next.

1   Click the **Line** tool ![icon] on the Draw toolbar.

2   Click on the drawing area where you want the line to start to pick the coordinates, or type the coordinates into the Command Line window.

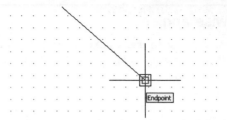

3 Drag across the screen and pick at the end of the line, or type the coordinates.

4 Drag and pick to draw another line, going on from the end-point, or type the next pair of coordinates. Repeat as needed.

5 Press [**Enter**] (or right-click) to stop drawing lines.

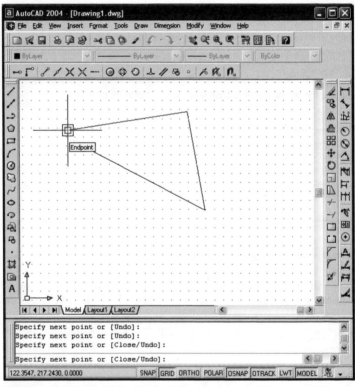

Figure 1.16 Drawing with the Line tool. The second square at the cross-hairs shows us that Object Snap is on and that the drawing point is over the end of an existing line.

Selecting and editing lines

Lines can be edited or deleted as needed at any time. First select them. Notice that each line is a separate object, even where they have been drawn in a continuous sequence to produce a shape.

To select a single line:

• Click on it.

To select several lines close to each other:

• Drag an outline to enclose all or part of the lines – the outline only has to touch a line to select it.

To select scattered lines:

• Hold [Shift] and click on each of the lines in turn.

A selected line is shown dashed with blue handles at each end and one at the mid-point.

To move a line:

• Click anywhere on the line and drag into the new position.

To stretch or change the angle:

• Place the pointer over an end handle and drag to change the angle or length.

To delete a line:

• Press [Delete] or click the **Eraser** tool .

Saving and closing files

Your work is precious and computers are not 100% reliable! Save your drawings early and save them often, so that if your machine crashes or is inadvertently turned off a recent copy of the file is available.

It only takes a few moments to save a drawing the first time. Resaving is even quicker – and you can have backup copies saved automatically.

To save a file for the first time:

1 Open the **File** menu and select **Save...**

2 Check that the folder in the **Save in** slot is the right one. If

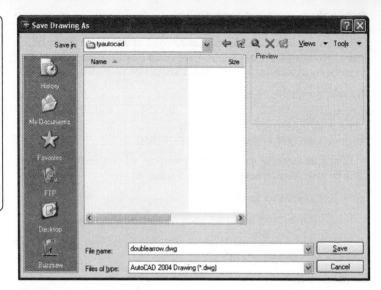

Figure 1.17 Saving a drawing file. Leave the **Files of type** at the default – the alternative formats are for special purposes.

not click the down arrow on the right of the box to select a higher level folder, or pick a subfolder from the main display.

3 Give the file a meaningful file name.

4 Click **OK**.

To resave a file:

♦ Select **Save** from the **File** menu, or click the **Save** button.

To use automatic saving:

1 Open the **Tools** menu and select **Options...**

2 Click on the **Open and Save** tab to open that panel.

3 In the **File Safety Precautions** area, tick the **Automatic save** checkbox and set the **Minutes between saves** value – something between 10 and 30 minutes will generally do.

4 Tick **Create backup copy with each save** if you want the extra security.

5 Tick **Full-time CRC validation** if you are having problems saving files successfully – this will check that an uncorrupted copy is stored on the disk.

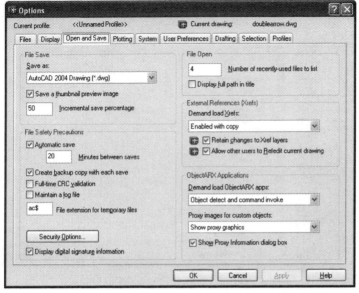

Figure 1.18 Setting the save options. We will be looking at more of the tabs in the Options dialog box later in the book.

6 Switch to the **Files** tab and double-click on the **Automatic Save File Location** entry to find out where the files are stored.

7 Click **OK** to close the **Options** dialog box.

Opening files

You can have any number of files open at once in AutoCAD – which can be very useful as it means that you can easily copy material from one to another.

To open a file:

1 Open the **File** menu and select **Open...**

2 At the **Select File** dialog box, browse through to the folder in the **Look in** slot.

3 Click on a file and look at its preview to check that it is the right one.

4 Click **Open**.

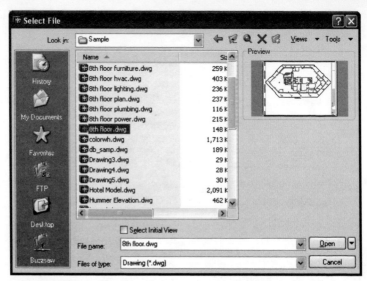

Figure 1.19 Opening a file. The Preview can help to identify files.

To move between open files:

• Open the **Window** menu and select the name of the file.

To close files:

• Open the **File** menu and select **Close**. If the file has not been saved recently, you will be prompted to save it.

Browse the samples

If you have not already done so, explore the sample files – find them in the Program Files/AutoCAD2004/Sample folder.

Exercises

1 Use the Line tool to draw these three objects. Use snap to grid for the first, simple coordinates for the second and relative coordinates for the third.

(1) 120,160; 280,160; 280,140; 120,140; 120,160

(2) 50,150; 120,200; 120,100; 50,150

(3) 280,200; @70,-50; @-70,-50; @0,100

What shape do you have? These lines should have produced a large double-headed arrow.

2 Use polar coordinates to draw these two objects.

(1) 10,100; @25<45; @50<0; @25<315; @50<270; @25<180; @25<0; @25<315; @50<270; @25<225; @50<180; @25<135; [Enter]

(2) 200,200; @25<135; @50<180; @25<225; @137<270; @25<315; @50<0; @25<45; @50<90; @25<135; @67<180; [Enter]

You should have the digits 3 and 6. Draw 5 to the same scale with its top right corner at 320,300.

Summary

• The AutoCAD window has a Command Line window below the main working space.

• There are nearly 30 toolbars. These can be turned on and off as required, and docked at the top or sides of the window, or left floating anywhere on screen.

• The right mouse button can be set to act as an [Enter] keypress. If the mouse has a wheel, it can be used for zooming and panning around the working space.

• You can pick coordinates with the mouse – Snap and Object Snap will enable you to do this more accurately.

• The drawing is created in model space, but is arranged for printed output in paper space.

• You can zoom in and out with the Zoom tools.

• Coordinates can be typed into the Command Line, as simple, relative or polar coordinates.

• The Line tool is used for drawing straight lines. A series of lines can be drawn at one time, with the end of one being the start of the next.

• Lines can be selected individually, or in groups. Once selected they can be edited or deleted.

• Drawing files should be saved regularly to guard against loss of work.

• When opening files, the preview can help to identify them.

02

the drawing tools

In this chapter you will learn:

- about the drawing tools
- how to set options
- how to select and edit objects

The Draw menu and the toolbar

The first thing you should learn about the drawing tools is that the toolbar only holds a selection of them. For the full set, you have to use the Draw menu, or the Command window.

The second thing to note is that several of the tools have options which give you an extra level of control over the shape or appearance of the object.

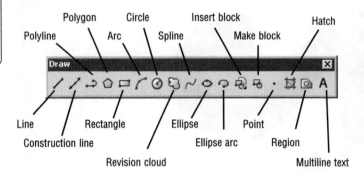

The Draw toolbar

Not all of the Draw tools are covered here. We used the Line tool in Chapter 1; we will look at the other drawing tools in Chapter 3, Hatch in Chapter 5 and Multiline text in Chapter 6. The Revision Cloud can be used to draw scalloped outlines around areas, and I will leave you to experiment with that.

Rectangles

The Rectangle tool is one of the simplest to use.

1 Click the **Rectangle** tool ▭.

2 Pick or type the coordinates of a corner.

3 Drag and pick at the opposite corner, or type its coordinates.

Rectangles are always drawn parallel to the axes. If you want one at an angle, rotate it afterwards (see page 55).

- A rectangle can be drawn square, but it may be easier to create squares using the Polygon tool.

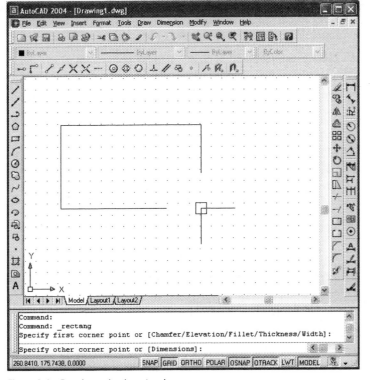

Figure 2.1 Drawing a simple rectangle.

Rectangle options

When the command first starts – before the first point has been defined – you are offered these options:

- **Chamfer** cuts off the corner at an angle. It takes two chamfer distances. If these are the same, the angle is 45°. If they are different, the effect is as shown below.

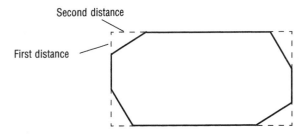

Second distance

First distance

- ◆ **Elevation** is the distance *above* the drawing surface. Most tools draw flat on the surface unless you type in the z coordinates. The effect is, of course, only visible in 3D views.

- ◆ **Fillet** gives rounded corners. You set the radius of the arc.

- ◆ **Thickness** adds a third dimension to the rectangle, so that the lines become blocks. This is only visible in 3D views.

- ◆ **Width** sets the width of the line. The default is 0, which shows as a hairline on the drawing.

After specifying the first point, you can use the **Dimension** option to define the rectangle by its length and width, rather than giving the coordinates of the opposite corner.

The options are all set in much the same way:

1 Type the first letter of the name, e.g. this selects Chamfer:

Specify first corner point or
[Chamfer/Elevation/Fillet/Thickness/Width]: c

2 Type a value or press [**Enter**] to accept the offered default, e.g. after selecting the Chamfer option:

Specify first chamfer distance for rectangles<0.000>:5
Specify second chamfer distance for rectangles<5.000>:10

AutoCAD options

When you are setting an option, AutoCAD will offer you the current value – if this is what you want, press [Enter] to accept it. Option values remain current in a drawing until changed. If you draw a rectangle at an elevation of 50, the next one will also be up there unless you reset the Elevation.

Examples

The four rectangles in Figure 2.2 are all basically the same size, but have these different options set.

1 Chamfer, first distance 20, second distance 10

2 Elevation, 40 and Width, 5.

3 Thickness, 50.

4 Fillet, radius 20 and Thickness, 25

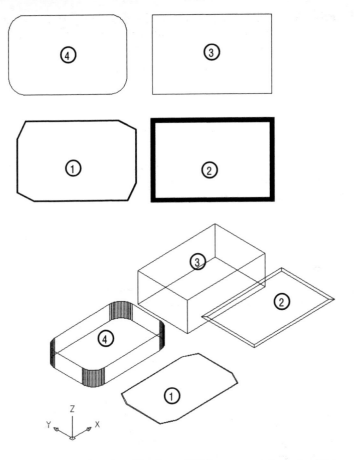

Figure 2.2 Rectangle options. Elevation and Thickness can only be see in a 3D view – the lower image is seen in the **View > 3D Views > SW Isometric** display.

Point and type

Combine the visual display of drawing with a mouse or other pointing device and the accuracy of typed coordinates. Use the mouse to draw your lines so that you can see the image develop, but instead of picking the endpoints, type the coordinates using the values in the Status bar as a guide.

Circles

The **Circle** tool is another very simple one.

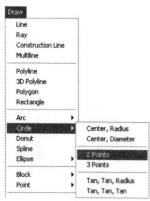

1 Click the **Circle** tool 🖉.

2 Pick or type the centre coordinates.

3 Type or drag and pick to set the radius

However, there are several variations on the **Draw** menu.

Point to **Circle** and you will see that a circle can be drawn in six ways:

- **Center, Radius** works the same way as the **Circle** tool.

- **Center, Diameter** is almost identical, though less intuitive to draw as the diameter indicator extends beyond the circle.

  The other four variations allow you to construct circles that meet up with two or more objects.

- With the **2 Points** option, you pick or type two points which will form the ends of a diameter.

- With **3 Points**, you specify any three points that the circle must touch.

- With **Tan, Tan, Radius** you specify two lines that the circle must touch without intersecting (i.e. the tangent points) and the radius of the circle.

- For the **Tan, Tan, Tan** option you need to specify three tangent points for the circle.

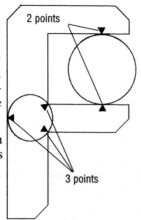

Figure 2.3 Drawing circles using the 2 points and 3 points methods.

Construction lines

Construction lines can help you to place and align objects. The lines extend the full width of the working space – and beyond – and are defined by specifying two points on the line. If several lines are drawn at one time, they all pass through the first point.

1 Click the **Construction line** tool.

2 Pick or type the coordinates to specify the first point.

3 Specify the second point.

4 Repeat **3** to define other lines passing through the first point.

5 Press [**Enter**] to end.

6 Start again from **1** to draw additional lines that do not pass through the first point.

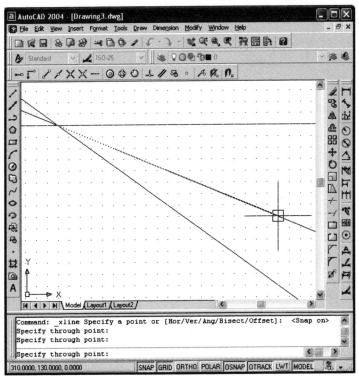

Figure 2.4 Drawing construction lines.

Polygons

A polygon is a shape with any number of equal sides. You can use the Polygon tool to create squares, triangles, pentagons, hexagons or whatever – any regular shape of up to 1024 sides!

Polygons can be defined in three ways:

* By the position and size of one edge – as all the other edges will be the same length this is enough to define the polygon.

* By the centre and the radius of a circle that it could be circumscribed around – i.e. the distance to the midpoint of an edge.

* By the centre and the radius of the circle that it could be inscribed in – i.e. the distance to a vertex.

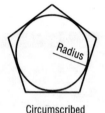

Circumscribed

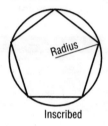

Inscribed

To define a polygon by an edge:

1 Click the **Polygon** tool ⬡.

2 Type the number of sides required.

3 Type 'E' to select Edge mode.

4 Specify the point at one end of an edge.

5 Drag to draw the line – the polygon, based on this, will take shape. Pick or type the coordinates to specify the endpoint.

To define a polygon by its centre and radius:

1 Click the **Polygon** tool ⬡ and type the number of sides.

2 Specify the centre point.

3 Type 'I' to select Inscribed, or 'C' for Circumscribed mode.

4 Type the radius.

Or

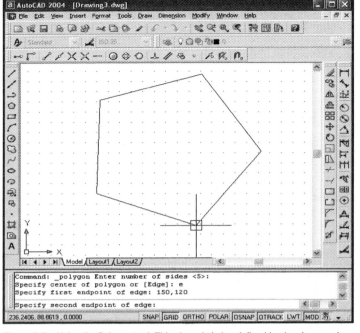

Figure 2.5 Using the Polygon tool. This shape is being defined by drawing an edge.

5 Use the mouse to drag the polygon to size and rotate it as required, clicking when it is in the right position.

Arcs

There are a dozen ways to draw an arc. The one linked to the **Arc** tool creates an arc from the start, end and another point anywhere else on the arc. The arc will be drawn clockwise or anticlockwise, depending upon the position of the points. In all the other modes the arcs are drawn *anticlockwise* – keep this in mind when specifying start or end points.

To draw an arc from three points:

1 Click the **Arc** tool *C*.

2 Specify the start point.

3 Specify another point anywhere on the arc – a straight line will (temporarily) link it to the start point.

4 Specify the end point.

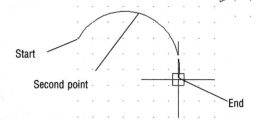

Start

Second point

End

The **Arc** command variations use different combinations of the seven points or measurements shown here, e.g. Start, Centre and End, or Start, End and Angle. Note that only three of these values – and it can be any three – are needed to define an arc.

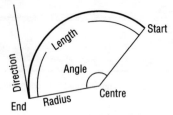

Length

Direction

Angle

Start

End   Radius   Centre

• The *direction* is that of the tangent to the arc at the start point.

To draw an Arc:

1 Open the **Draw** menu and point to **Arc**.

2 Select the Arc option that best fits with the drawing that you have developed to that stage.

3 Type the values or pick the co-ordinates to define the points, angle or length in the appropriate order.

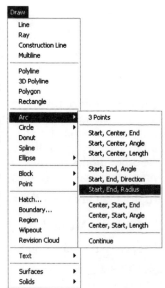

Draw
Line
Ray
Construction Line
Multiline

Polyline
3D Polyline
Polygon
Rectangle

Arc   ▶   3 Points
Circle   ▶
Donut   Start, Center, End
Spline   Start, Center, Angle
Ellipse   ▶   Start, Center, Length

Block   ▶   Start, End, Angle
Point   ▶   Start, End, Direction
                  Start, End, Radius
Hatch...
Boundary...   Center, Start, End
Region   Center, Start, Angle
Wipeout   Center, Start, Length
Revision Cloud
                  Continue
Text   ▶

Surfaces   ▶
Solids   ▶

Continuation lines

If you want to draw a tangent which continues directly on from the end of the arc, there is a simple way to do this:

1 Select the Line tool and press [Enter] to accept the end of the arc as the start point for the line.

2 Specify the length of the line only – AutoCAD will automatically set it to the arc's end angle.

Splines

This draws a continuous line with multiple curves. The line is defined largely by the points on the cusps of the curves. The curves at the start and end are defined separately afterwards.

To draw a spline:

1 Click on the **Spline** tool .

2 Click or type the coordinates to specify the start point.

3 Specify the points to locate the curves along the line.

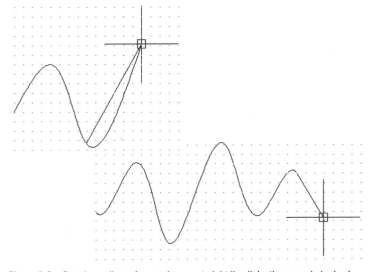

Figure 2.6 Drawing splines. As you draw, a straight line links the cross-hairs back to the previous point.

4 Press [**Enter**] at the end.

5 A straight line will appear, connecting to the start point. Move this to form the first curve. Repeat for the end curve.

Ellipses

An ellipse has two axes that cross at right angles. The shape is defined by the length of those axes, and their angle to the grid.

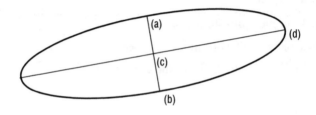

To define an ellipse:

1 Click on the **Ellipse** tool ⬤.

2 Specify the position of the startpoint of an axis (a).

3 Drag and pick or type the coordinates to set the length and angle of the axis (b).

4 Specify the length of the other axis, from the centre (c) to the edge (d) – its angle will be 90 degrees to the first.

The ⬤ tool is the same as the **Draw > Ellipse > Axis, End** option. The **Draw** menu also has an **Ellipse > Center** option. In this, the first point to be defined is the centre, and both axes are defined by specifying their length from the centre.

Ellipse arcs

An elipse arc is defined by first creating an ellipse, then marking the start and end angles of the arc within it. When setting these, remember that arcs are drawn anticlockwise.

1 Click on the **Ellipse Arc** tool ⬚.

2 Draw an ellipse as shown above.

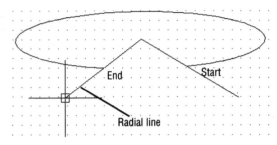

3 A radial line will appear. Type the start angle, or swing the radial line around the centre to point to the start, then click to pick the angle.

4 Type the angle or swing the line and pick the end angle.

Points

Points are mainly used to act as snap points to help in the construction of other objects. Their screen appearance depends upon the point style, and can be highly visible – which you may need when using them as guides – or totally invisible – so they don't intrude on the finished drawing. The default style is a single pixel.

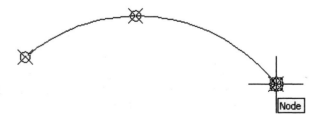

Figure 2.7   An arc being drawn using points as guides.

To place points:

1 Click the Point tool .

2 Type or pick its coordinates.

3 Repeat 2 to place more points as required.

4 Press [Escape] or select another tool to end.

To set the point style:

1 Open the **Format** menu and select **Point Style...**

2 Select a style.

3 If required, set the size, either as relative to the screen or in absolute units.

4 Click **OK**.

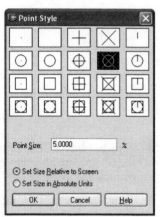

♦ The style will be applied to any existing points and to all that you draw from that time. Come back and change the style later to make the points more or less visible.

Polylines

The Polyline tool is used in basically the same way as the Line tool, but there are several differences in the result. The first is that even when used in a continuous sequence, Line-drawn lines are separate objects, but Polyline-drawn lines form a single object – clicking anywhere on a polyline selects the whole set. A polyline does not have to end back at the startpoint, but if it does, this creates a closed object which can be filled (Chapter 5).

The other differences arise from the greater flexibility of polylines. A polyline can be a straight line or an arc, and it can be of any thickness – and the thickness can taper from one end to the other. As a result, you can produce more or less any shape with the Polyline – we'll start with something simple, then go on to explore it.

1 Click the **Polyline** tool .

2 Click to pick the start of the first line or type the coordinates.

3 Drag and pick to draw the line, or type the coordinates of the endpoint. Repeat as necessary.

4 Press [**Enter**] (or right-click) to end.

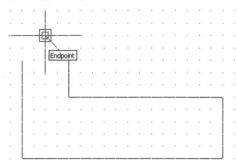

Figure 2.8   A simple polyline under construction.

Polyline options

Polyline has a number of options which can be selected when you see the prompt:

Specify next point or [Arc/Close/Halfwidth/Length/Undo/Width]

Arc: draws an arc, instead of a straight line. Unless you specify otherwise, the arc will be such that the previous line would meet it at a tangent. In practice, this means that you can use it to draw rounded corners and ends without further specification.

In arc-drawing mode, there are the additional options: **Angle**, **Center**, **Direction**, **Line**, **Radius**, **Second point** and **End point**.

Line reverts to line-drawing mode; the rest are used for specifying the position and angle of the arc. The simplest are **Direction**, which sets the tangent direction – you can see this in the example below – and **Second point** and **End point**, which are used as they are with the **Arc** tool.

Close: draws a line from the last endpoint to the start of the polyline, creating a closed shape. This can be filled (Chapter 5).

Halfwidth: is – literally – half the width of the line. Use it in exactly the same way as Width (but at half the value!).

Length: draws a straight line of the given length, continuing at the same angle as the previous line or as a tangent from an arc.

Undo: undoes the last command within the polyline. This is very useful, as things can go wrong with this complex feature, and it would be a shame to have to start again from scratch because of one error.

Width: the start and end widths are set separately, and if they are different, the line's thickness will smoothly taper from one to the other over its length.

To set polyline options:

1 Type the first (and sometimes the second) letter of the name, e.g. this selects Arc drawing mode, then the Center option:

> Specify next point or [Arc/Halfwidth/Length/Undo/Width]: a
> Specify endpoint of arc or [Angle/CEnter/Direction/Halfwidth/
> Line/Radius/Second ptUndo/Width]: ce

2 Type a value or press **[Enter]** to accept the offered default, e.g. after selecting the Width option:

> Specify starting width <1.000>: 5
> Specify ending width <5.000>: 25

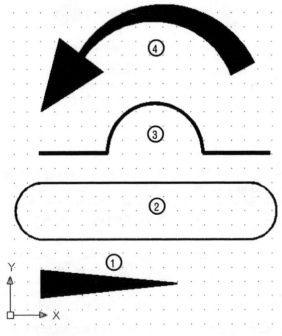

Figure 2.9 Examples of polylines.

The polylines in Figure 2.9 were produced by the following command sequences:

1 Start point: 50,50
  Option: Width, Starting 20, Ending 1
  Second point, @100,0
  [Enter]

2 Start point: 50,120
  Second point: 200,120
  Option: Arc
  Next point: 200,80
  Option: Line
  Next point: 50,80
  Option: Arc
  Next point: 50,120
  Close

3 Start point: 50, 140
  Option: Width, Starting 2, Ending 2
  Next point: 100,140
  Option: Arc
  Option: Direction, 90
  Next point: 170,140
  Option: Line
  Next point: 220,140

4 Start point: 200,200
  Option: Width, Starting 20, Ending 5
  Option: Arc
  Option: Direction, 105
  Next point: 80,210
  Option: Width, Starting 40, Ending 0
  Option: Line
  Next point: 50,170

Selecting and editing objects

To select a single object:

♦ Click on one of its lines.

To select several objects close to each other:

♦ Drag an outline to enclose all or touch on the objects.

To select scattered objects:

♦ Hold [**Shift**] and click on each of the objects in turn.

A selected object is shown in dashed lines with blue handles at each vertex. Circles and ellipses also have a handle at the centre.

To move an object:

♦ Click on any line – not a handle – and drag into position.

To delete an object:

♦ Select it and press [**Delete**] or click the Eraser 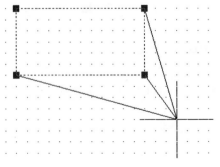.

Adjusting the shape

You can adjust the shape of an object by dragging its handles. The effect varies with the nature of the shape, and this may not be the best way to edit an object. In Chapter 3 we will look at the Modify tools, which can be used to manipulate objects in different ways; and in Chapter 4 you will meet the Properties panel, where you can define the positions of vertices accurately.

To move a vertex (distorting the shape):

1 Click on the handle and drag. The new position of the vertex and the length and angles of the lines joining at it will be shown.

2 Release the mouse when you are happy with the shape.

To change the width or length of a rectangle:

1 Hold down [**Shift**].

2 Click on the vertices at the opposite ends of a side.

3 Drag on either vertex to move the line smoothly in or out. It will remain at right angles to the adjacent sides.

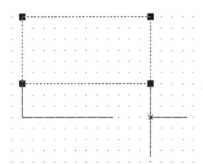

4 Release the button to fix the new width/length.

♦ You can use the same technique to move any number of vertices of a polygon or polyline at once. The vertices will all move in the same direction and angle. You must hold [**Shift**] before you start to select the vertices.

To change the size of a circle:

1 Click on one of the quadrant handles (those on the perimeter).

2 Drag in or out to set the size – the circle will not be distorted.

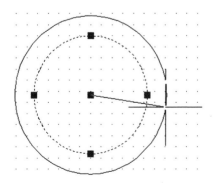

3 Release the button when the circle is the right size.

To change the shape of an ellipse:

1 Click on the handle at the end of one of the axes.

2 Drag in or out to change its length (and the shape of the ellipse).

3 Release the button when the axis is the right length.

4 Repeat for the other axis if required.

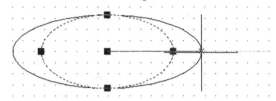

Exercises

1 Use the Rectangle and Circle tools to draw this pattern.

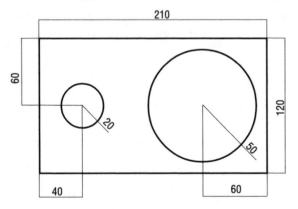

2 Use the Rectangle tool to draw the next object. The outside rectangle has a fillet of 20. Remember to reset the fillet to 0 before starting to draw the inside rectangle.

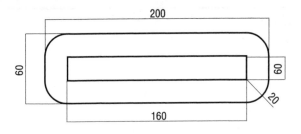

3 Use the Polygon and Line tools to draw this. (Tip: use object snap and polar coordinates to define the lines that radiate out from the polygon.)

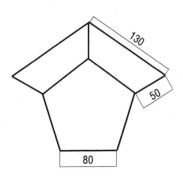

4 Construct this shape using the Polyline tool – it will actually take several polylines to create the whole outline.

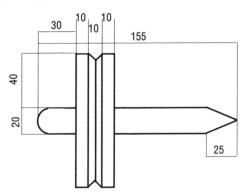

Summary

- Most drawing tools can be selected from the Draw toolbar. The Draw menu has all of these and more.

- To draw a rectangle, you just give the coordinates of two opposite corners.

- Circles can be drawn by giving the centre and radius, or by specifying points that they must intersect or meet.

- Construction lines can be added to help align objects.

- Polygons can have anything from 3 to 1024 sides. They can be defined by an edge, or by the position and size of their inscribed or circumscribed circles.

- There are a dozen ways to draw an arc – experiment with them so that you are able to use the most appropriate way in different situations.

- A spline is a curved line. It is defined by the cusps of its curves and the tangents of its ends.

- An ellipse has two axes at right angles to each other, and is defined by the length of those axes.

- To create an ellipse arc, you first draw an ellipse, then mark the start and end angles of the arc.

- Points can be used to help to draw other objects.

- A polyline has a number of lines, which are treated as a single unit. The polyline command has several options. You can set its width, which can change from one end to the other; draw a straight line or an arc; undo the previous segment, to correct an error; or join the end back to the start to create a closed shape.

- Objects can be selected and deleted in the same way as lines. You can adjust the shape and size of objects by dragging on the selection handles.

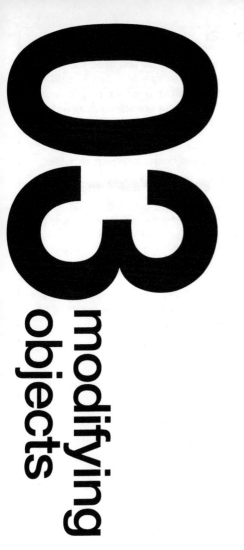

03

**modifying
objects**

In this chapter you will learn:

- about the modify tools
- how to copy, move and rotate objects
- how to trim or extend lines
- how to chamfer and fillet angles

The Modify toolbar

The Modify toolbar contains all key tools you need for manipulating objects. Many of them work in similar ways, so that once you have mastered one tool, the next is easier to get to grips with. Notice in particular how objects are selected, and the use of a base point. Learn about these first with the Erase and Copy tools.

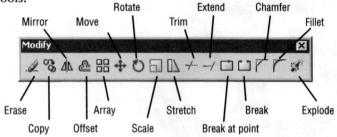

Rotate · Extend · Chamfer

Mirror · Move · Trim · Fillet

Erase · Array · Stretch · Break · Explode

Copy · Offset · Scale · Break at point

Erase

This is the simplest of the Modify tools.

1 Select the objects you want to remove.

2 Click the **Erase** tool .

Or

1 Click the **Erase** tool .

2 Select the objects you want to remove.

3 Press [**Enter**] or right-click to tell AutoCAD that you have finished selecting objects.

Selecting objects for modifying

Objects can be selected before or after clicking the tool. It is simplest to select them first. If you start the tool first, AutoCAD goes into a 'select object' mode. You can then select objects by dragging over them or [Shift]-clicking, or a combination of both – but AutoCAD will stay in its 'select object' mode until you press [Enter] to signal that you have got them all. Watch out for this. If you are used to working in other Windows applications, it does not feel intuitive.

Copy

The standard Windows Copy and Paste technique works perfectly well, but it is worth knowing about the Copy command as it can give you better control when you place the copies.

After selecting the objects, you must specify a base point. The copy is then located by giving the position of its base point. This allows very accurate positioning.

By default, only one copy is made at a time. If several are wanted, switch on the multiple option at the start of the command.

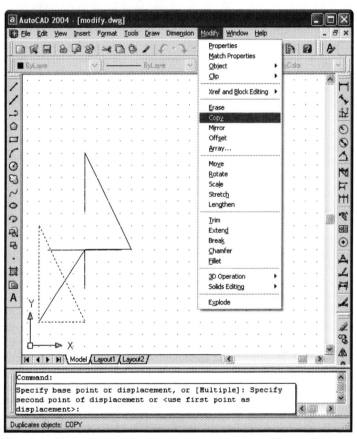

Figure 3.1 Making a copy – a line joins the base points of the original (dotted outline) and the copy while it is being placed. Note that the Modify menu has a few more commands than the toolbar.

To copy:

1 Select the object(s).

2 Click the **Copy** tool 🔧.

Or

♦ Click the **Copy** tool 🔧, select the objects and press **[Enter]**.

3 If multiple copies are needed, type 'M' in the Command Line.

4 Pick a base point in or near the objects.

5 Pick where you want to place the base point of the copy.

6 In Multiple mode, place the other copies then press **[Enter]**.

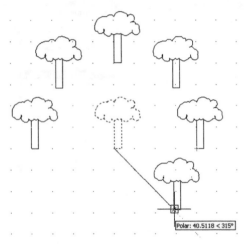

Figure 3.2 Making multiple copies. Here polar tracking (press [F10] to toggle it on or off) has been turned on to help place the copies. It shows the distance and angle from the last point.

Mirror

The Mirror tool produces a mirror image, allowing you to create a symmetrical object by drawing only half of it – or even a smaller fraction. You place the mirror line by picking two points on it – the line will swivel after the first point has been set, and you will be able to see how the reflection will look and where it will appear. Picking the second point fixes the line and creates the new drawing – the original can be kept or removed as desired.

To create a mirror image:

1 Select the object(s).

2 Click the **Mirror** tool 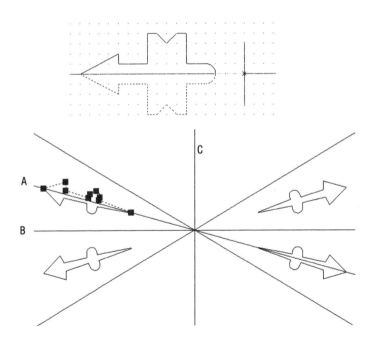.

Or

♦ Click the **Mirror** tool , select the objects and press [**Enter**].

3 Pick the coordinates of one point on the mirror line.

4 Pick the second point to fix the line.

5 The Command Line will prompt:

Delete source objects? [Yes/No] <N> :

Type 'Y' to delete the object, or press [**Enter**] to accept the default (No).

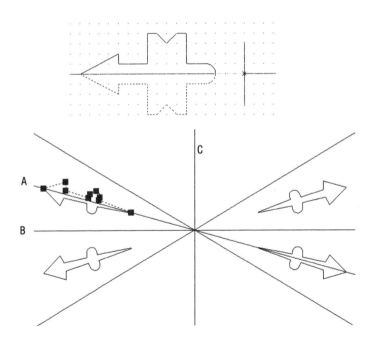

Figure 3.3 Mirrored objects. A simple reflection in the horizontal (top) and a multiple image created by mirroring the selected polyline first in the lines A, then B, then C (bottom).

Offset

Offset creates copies of an outline within or outside the source shape. It is unusual in that you cannot select an object first – you must start with the tool (or command) and specify the offset distance before selecting the object.

1 Select the **Offset** tool 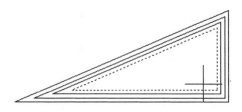.

2 Type the offset distance into the Command Line.

3 Click on the source object.

4 Click inside or outside of the object to tell AutoCAD whether to make an inner or outer offset.

5 Repeat step **4** to create more offsets of the same object, or go back to step **3** to select a new object.

6 Press [**Enter**] or right-click to end.

Figure 3.4 Creating offsets. Clicking at this point would create a new offset inside the original (dotted) shape.

Array

This creates a regularly spaced array of copies of an object. The array can be a rectangular grid or a polar pattern, radiating around a central point.

To create a rectangular array:

1 Select the object(s).

2 Click the **Array** tool ▦.

Or

• Click the **Array** tool ▦, select the objects and press [**Enter**].

3 Select the **Rectangular Array** option at the top of the **Array** dialog box.

4 Set the number of **Rows** and **Columns**.

5 Enter the **Row** and **Column offsets** – the distance between the same points on two copies.

6 The **Angle of array** tilts the array from the horizontal. Set a value if required.

7 Click **OK**.

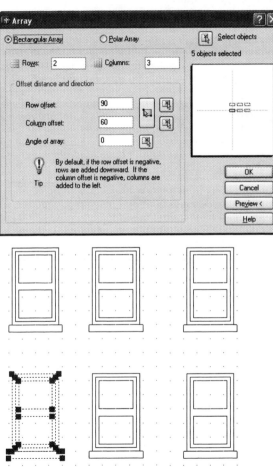

Figure 3.5 The array produced by the settings in the dialog box, based on the selected 'window frame' object.

To create a polar array:

1 Start as for a rectangular array, but selecting the **Polar Array** option in the **Array** dialog box.

2 Type the **Center point** coordinates, or click 🔳 and pick the point.

3 Set the **Total number of items** and the **Angle to fill**.

4 Tick or clear the **Rotate items as copied** checkbox on the bottom left, as required.

5 Click **OK**.

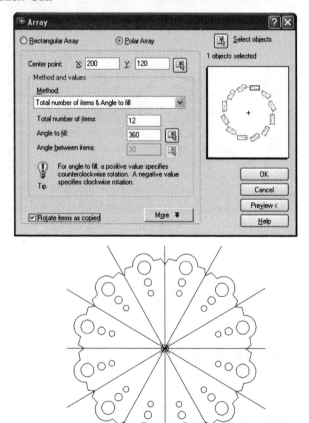

Figure 3.6 An example of a polar array.

Move

You can move an object by dragging. The main advantage of the Move tool is its greater accuracy. It also avoids the possibility of distorting an object by dragging on a handle, instead of a line.

1 Select the object(s).

2 Click the **Move** tool ⊹.

Or

◆ Click the **Move** tool ⊹, select the objects and press [**Enter**].

3 Pick a base point in or near the objects.

4 Type the coordinates or pick where you want to move the base point to.

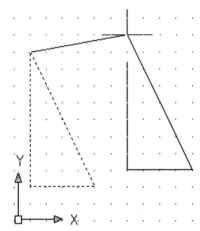

Figure 3.7 Moving an object.

Rotate

An object can be rotated about any point, either within its shape or elsewhere on screen.

1 Select the object(s).

2 Click the **Rotate** tool ◐.

Or

◆ Click the **Rotate** tool ◐, select the objects and press [**Enter**].

3 Type the coordinates or pick the point to rotate around.

4 Type the angle, or rotate the object with the mouse.

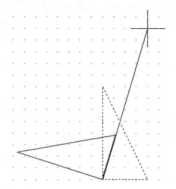

Figure 3.8 Rotating an object by dragging the guide line.

Scale

Scaling makes an object uniformly larger or smaller. It works by changing all the coordinates by the same factor and in relation to a given point. You can visualize it as projecting a shadow, and the size of a shadow depends upon the relative positions of the object and the light source.

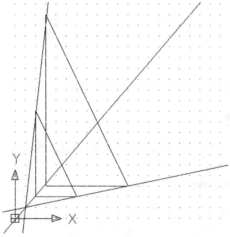

Figure 3.9 Scaling changes the size and position of an object relative to a given point. This shows a scale factor of 2.

1 Select the object(s).

2 Click the **Scale** tool ▣.

Or

* Click the **Scale** tool ▣, select the objects and press [**Enter**].

3 Pick a base point within the object to change its size without moving it, or outside to change the size and position.

4 Type the scale factor in at the Command Line – the values are usually too small to set accurately with a mouse.

Stretch

This will take part of an object and move it in relation to the rest to stretch – or shrink – the overall shape. You could do the same job by selecting the handles at one end and dragging them, but this is a little simpler.

As with the **Offset** command, you must start **Stretch** before you select the objects. Selection is done using a 'crossing window' – a dotted rectangle that appears when you drag across the screen. Any object that is inside or is touched by this window is selected.

1 Select the **Stretch** tool ▣.

2 Click to fix one corner of the crossing window.

3 Drag the window over the objects you want to select, and click to fix its other corner.

4 Press [**Enter**] to end the select object routine.

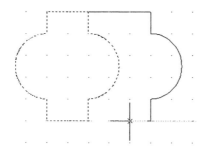

Figure 3.10 Using stretch to lengthen a shape.

5 Type the coordinates or pick a point in the selected area.

6 Type the new coordinates or drag the point to where you want to stretch it.

Trim and Extend

Rather than draw exactly the right shape or length of lines, it is sometimes simpler to draw to the approximate length or shape, and then trim off the excess or extend lines to make an exact fit.

You can trim to where a line meets an existing line, or add new lines to act as the 'cutting edge'. Similarly, when extending lines, an existing or a temporary line can act as the boundary edge.

To trim a line or shape:

1 If necessary, draw the cutting edge lines.

2 Click the **Trim** tool .

3 Select the lines to act as the cutting edge, then press [**Enter**].

4 Click on the lines or shapes where they project beyond the cutting edge.

5 Repeat to trim other lines or shapes and press [**Enter**] to end.

6 If the cutting edge line has no other purpose, delete it.

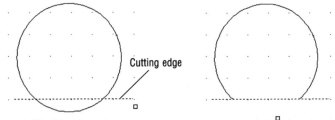

Figure 3.11 Trimming a shape.

To extend lines:

1 If necessary, draw the boundary edge lines.

2 Click the **Extend** tool .

3 Select the lines to act as the boundary edge and press [**Enter**].

4 Click on the lines to extend to meet the boundary edge.

5 Repeat to trim other lines or shapes. Press [**Enter**] to end.

6 If the boundary edge line has no other purpose, delete it.

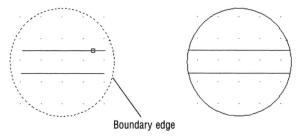

Boundary edge

Figure 3.12 Extending lines to meet a boundary edge.

Break

There are two versions of this tool. **Break** cuts a section out of a line or shape – use it for creating openings in solid outlines or as an alternative to **Trim**. **Break at point** cuts through a line or a shape, creating two lines though the ends still meet – use it to subdivide lines so that the sections can be manipulated separately or as an alternative to **Explode** (see page 63) to cut one line out of a polygon or polyline.

You must select the tool first in both versions.

To break a line:

1 Select the **Break** tool ▢.

2 Click on the line at the point where you want to break it – this selects the line and the break point.

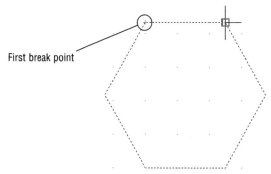

First break point

Figure 3.13 Setting the second break point in a selected shape.

3 Click where you want the second break point.

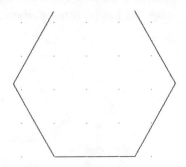

Figure 3.14 Break removes the line between the break points.

To break at a point:

1 Select the **Break at point** tool ▣.

2 Click on the line or shape to select it.

3 Click where you want the break point.

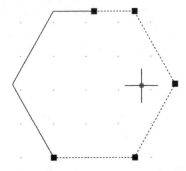

Figure 3.15 The shape will appear to be unchanged after setting a break point, but if you click on it, you will see that only one part will be selected.

Broken shapes

When a closed shape is cut, it also breaks at its first vertex, becoming two separate objects.

Chamfer

We met chamfer earlier as an option when drawing rectangles. The Chamfer tool does a similar job – it cuts off a corner at an angle. It works on a vertex of any shape or on any pair of lines that can intersect – though they do not have to actually meet or cross. The chamfer angle is determined by the distances along the first and second lines from the point of intersection – and which line is first or second depends on the order in which you select them.

For example, to chamfer this corner, we would set up the first chamfer distances as 5 and the second as 10, then select A as the first line and B as the second.

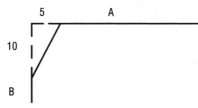

♦ The chamfer option on a rectangle applies to all four corners. The chamfer tool normally only cuts one corner at a time. The Multiple option will let you apply the same cut successively to any number of corners. The Polyline option will apply the current chamfer settings to every angle in a polyline object.

1 Click the **Chamfer** tool 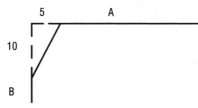.

2 The current chamfer distances will be shown in the Command Line. If these are OK, go to step **5**.

3 If you want to chamfer several corners, type 'U' to turn on the Multiple option.

4 Type 'D' to select the Distance option.

5 Enter the first then the second chamfer distances.

```
(TRIM mode) Current chamfer Dist1 = 10.0000, Dist2 = 5.0000
Select first line or [Polyline/Distance/Angle/Trim/Method/mUltiple]: d
Specify first chamfer distance <10.0000>: 5
Specify second chamfer distance <5.0000>:
```

6 Select the line to apply the first chamfer distance to.

7 Select the second line.

8 Repeat steps **6** and **7** for other corners if in Multiple mode.

Fillet

This is similar to but simpler than **Chamfer**. It will round off any corner, or draw an arc to join a pair of lines that intersect or could intersect if extended.

- If the lines do not meet, and the radius of the fillet will not produce an arc big enough to join them, the lines will be extended to connect to the arc.

- If the lines intersect, the parts of the lines beyond the fillet arc will normally be trimmed. If you want to retain them, turn the Trim option off.

- The Multiple and Polyline options are the same as in **Chamfer**.

1 Click the **Fillet** tool [icon].

2 Check the current settings.

3 Type 'R' then the value to change the Radius.

4 Type 'T', then the setting if you want to change the Trim mode.

5 Type 'U' if you want to turn on the Multiple option.

6 Select the two lines to fillet – the order is irrelevant.

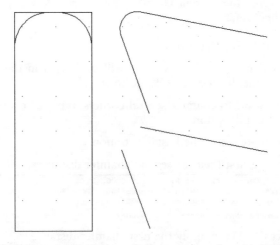

Figure 3.16 Using the Fillet tool – applied to two corners of a rectangle with the Trim option turned off (left); two lines joined by a fillet, before (below right) and after (top right).

Explode

This will break up a polyline, polygon or rectangle into its component lines. Use it if you need to delete or change the properties of one line in a compound object without affecting the rest.

It can also be used to break up blocks (see Chapter 8) into their components.

1 Select the object(s).

2 Click the **Explode** tool .

Or

• Click the **Explode** tool, select the objects and press [**Enter**].

An explosion is irreversible! If you need to reassemble the lines into a unit so that it can be handled more conveniently, you can make them into a block – which we will look at in Chapter 8.

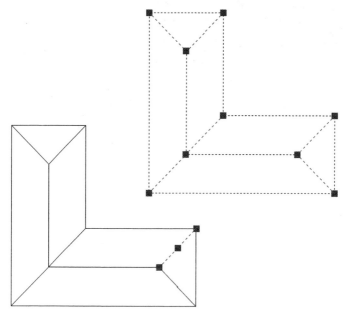

Figure 3.17 A polyline before (top) and after (bottom) exploding. In the exploded drawing, it is possible to select – and edit – one line without affecting the rest.

Exercises

1 Draw a right-angled triangle, 80 units high by 40 wide. Mirror it along its hypotenuse, keeping the original. Select and rotate the two triangles together, picking the lower end of the hypotenuse as the base point, to produce the 'arrowhead' effect shown here.

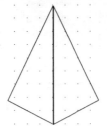

2 Draw a circle of radius 50 units. Using the Offset tool, create four more circles within it, each 10 units smaller than the next. Draw a square of 70 units, with its top left corner at the centre of the circles. Use this as a cutting edge to trim the lower right quadrants from the circle, to produce this image.

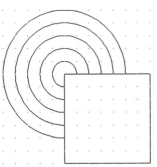

3 Draw a house image, based on a rectangle of 80 by 60 units, with a roof, windows and a door. Use the Scale tool to reduce it to half size. Create eight copies of it with a polar array, setting the centre of the array approximately 30 units down and to the right of the lower right corner of the house.

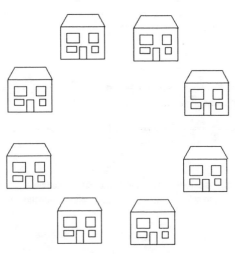

Summary

*   The main tools for editing and manipulating objects can be found on the Modify toolbar.

*   With most modify tools, you can either select the objects before the tool, or vice versa.

*   Press [Delete] or use the Erase tool to remove unwanted objects.

*   The Copy tool gives you better control over the placing of copies than the standard Windows Copy and Paste.

*   An object can be reflected in any mirror plane.

*   The Offset tool allows you to create copies of a shape within or outside the original.

*   A whole set of copies can be created at once with the Array tool. They can be arranged in a rectangluar or polar pattern.

*   An object can be rotated around any point, within or beyond its boundaries.

*   Scaling changes the size and position of an object in relation to a base point.

*   The stretch routine allows you to make part of an object longer, without affecting the rest.

*   Lines can be cut to length with the Trim tool, or extended to intersect a boundary. They can also be broken at a point, or by removing a section.

*   The point of an intersection can be chamfered or filleted.

*   A polyline, rectangle, polygon or block can be exploded into its components.

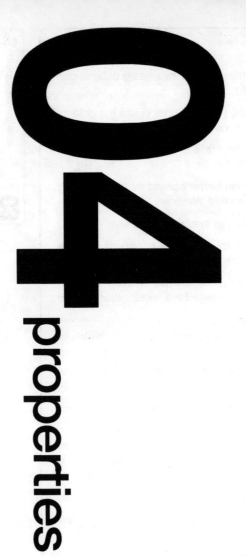

04

properties

In this chapter you will learn:

- about the properties of lines and shapes
- how to format lines from the Properties toolbar options
- how to display and to use the Properties palette

The Properties toolbar

You can set the type, weight and colour of lines with the options in the drop-down lists on the **Properties** toolbar, and add to the range of available settings, change the defaults and adjust other aspects of these properties through the commands on the **Format** menu.

ByLayer and ByBlock

At the top of each of the line properties drop-down list are the options ByLayer and ByBlock. You can set the default colour, type and weight for each layer of a drawing – see Chapter 7 for more on layers. An object with its properties set to ByLayer takes the colour, type and weight of the layer settings, and so will change if the defaults are changed, and if copied or inserted into another drawing will take the properties of the layer into which it is placed.

The current settings in the Properties toolbar are applied to new objects as they are drawn. These may be different from the defaults for the layer. For example, if you defined the layer to draw lines in red, but then set the colour option to blue, subsequent new lines would be drawn in blue.

If you create a block with its properties set to ByBlock, when it is inserted into a new drawing, it will take its colour, type and weight from the current selection in the Properties toolbar, or the ByLayer defaults if the properties have not been individually set.

If you want an object or block to retain its properties when copied or inserted, each must be set individually and not using either ByLayer or ByBlock.

Lineweight

By default, lines are 0.01" (0.25mm) wide, but the lineweights can be anything from 0.0mm up to 2.11mm. By default, however, the thickness is not shown on screen. AutoCAD normally draws all lines one pixel wide, rather than showing them at their actual widths, as this allows the screen to be redrawn much faster – remember that the displayed width is relative to the zoom level, so there is quite a lot of extra processing involved. If required, you can turn on the lineweight display.

• On simple drawings, screen redrawing is not significantly slower when lineweights are displayed, but the more complex the drawing, the more you will notice the difference.

To control the lineweight display:

1 Open the **Format** menu and select **Lineweights…**

2 At the **Lineweight Settings** dialog box, tick (or clear) the **Display Lineweight** checkbox.

3 Set the **Adjust Display Scale** slider to the centre or towards the **Min** end – the lower it is, the faster the system can work.

4 Pick a new value from the **Lineweights** list to set the Current Lineweight, if required.

5 Pick a new value from the **Default** drop-down list if you want to set a different default value.

6 Click **OK**.

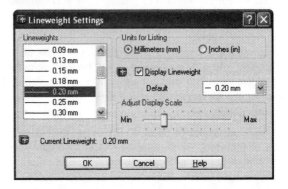

Figure 4.1 Changing the default value will change the weight of any existing lines that have not had their lineweight set. Changing the current lineweight only affects lines drawn from that point on.

To set the lineweight:

1 Select the object(s) to format.

2 Drop down the **Lineweights** list on the Properties toolbar.

3 Select a recently-used weight from the top of the list, or scroll down to select a new value.

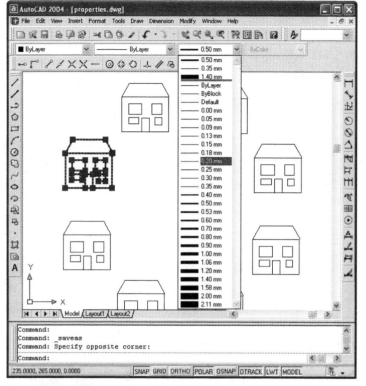

Figure 4.2 Setting the lineweight for a group of objects.

Linetype

If you want to indicate hidden lines or a different type of connection, e.g. wiring or plumbing in a building plan, you could use a different linetype.

Initially there are only three linetypes available from the drop-down list in the Properties toolbar, but more are easily added.

To add a linetype:

1 Open the Linetypes drop-down list and click **Other...**

Or

◆ Open the **Format** menu and select **Linetypes...**

2 At the **Linetype Manager** dialog box, click **Load…**

3 Scroll through the list and select a linetype.

4 If you want to add more types at the same time, hold down [**Ctrl**] and click on the others.

5 Click **OK** when you have selected your type(s).

6 Click **OK** to close the **Linetype Manager** dialog box.

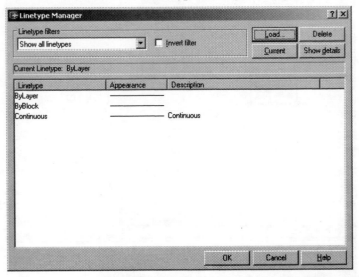

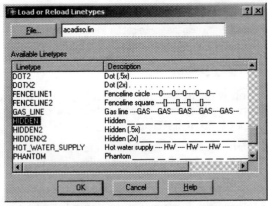

Figure 4.3 Loading a new line type. Note that as well as a range of dots and dashes, there are types for specific purposes.

To set the linetype:

1 Select the line(s) to be formatted.

2 Open the **Linetype** drop-down list.

3 If there is a suitable type, click on it.

Or

4 Click **Other...** to add a new line type to the list.

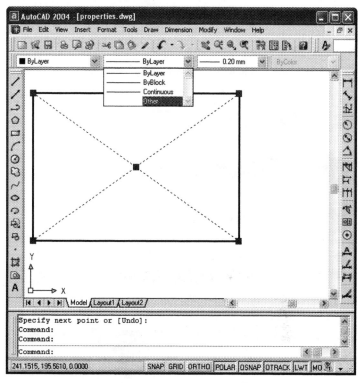

Figure 4.4 Setting the linetype.

Line colour

Line colour is also changed through a list on the Properties toolbar, and again there is initially a limited selection. If more or different colours are needed, they can be added via a very comprehensive routine.

To set the line colour:

1 Select the line(s) to be formatted.

2 Open the **Color** drop-down list.

3 If there is a suitable colour, click on it.

To add more colours to the list:

1 Click **Select Color...** at the bottom of the list.

Or

♦ Open the **Format** menu and select **Color...**

2 Go to a tab and select a colour.

♦ On the **Index Color** tab, select from AutoCAD's own set.

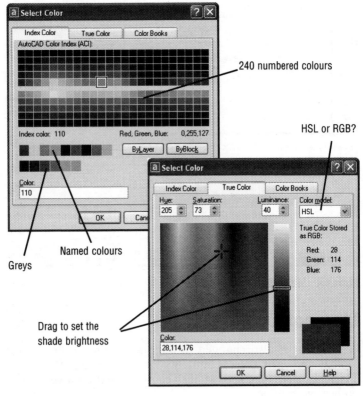

240 numbered colours

HSL or RGB?

Named colours

Greys

Drag to set the shade brightness

Figure 4.5 The Index Color and True Color tabs.

- On the **True Color** tab, in the **Color model** slot at the top right, choose the **HSL** (Hue, Saturation, Luminance) or **RGB** (Red, Green, Blue), then set the values in the number fields or on the colour spectrum.

- On the **Color Books** tab, you can select industry standard colours from the Pantone or RAL ranges.

The Properties palette

The Properties palette can be used to view or change the colour, line type, position, dimensions and other properties of objects.

The properties are grouped into sets, and for most objects there are three sets: *General*, *Geometry* and *Miscellaneous*, though what is in the palette depends upon what type of object – or types of objects – are selected at the time.

Almost all objects have the same *General* properties – colour, linetype, lineweight and the like. The *Geometry* properties vary according to how the object is drawn – a line is basically defined by its start and end coordinates; a circle by its centre and radius; an arc has the same properties as a circle, plus more to define its start and end. The simpler objects have no *Miscellaneous* properties.

If several objects are selected, the palette will only include those properties which they all share. But see for yourself…

The display of the properties in each set can be turned on and off by clicking the chevrons at the right of the title bars.

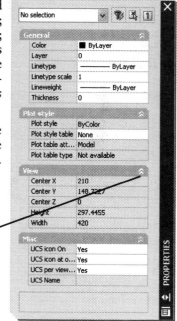

Figure 4.6 The Properties palette when no object is selected.

To open the Properties palette:

1 Click the 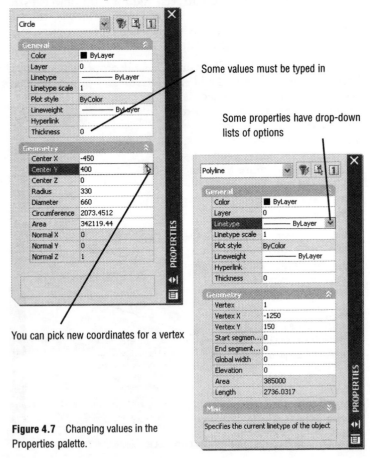 button on the Standard toolbar.

- When no object is selected, the palette shows the current settings for the drawing.

2 Click on an object in the drawing area to see its properties in the palette.

If a property is shown on a white background, it can be changed – exactly how depends on the nature of the property.

To change a property:

1 Click on the property to select it.

Some values must be typed in

Some properties have drop-down lists of options

You can pick new coordinates for a vertex

Figure 4.7 Changing values in the Properties palette.

2 If it is a simple number, e.g. thickness, type in the new value.

3 If it is a coordinate, a pick arrow 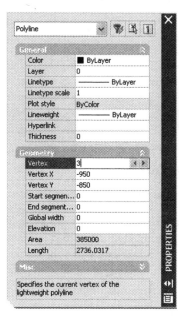 will appear on the right of the field. Click on this, then pick a new position for the vertex in the drawing area.

4 If a down arrow appears at the right of the field, click on this to drop down a list of options and select a value from there.

5 Polylines have a **Vertex** property – the number of the current vertex. This allows you to work round the vertices, and to view or adjust their coordinates. Use the arrows on the right of the field to change the number.

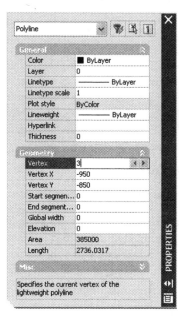

Figure 4.8 Changing the current vertex in a polyline.

Multiple selections

If you select several objects at once, you can set the same shared property for all of the objects in a single operation – and properties are set in the usual way.

The selected objects are grouped by type, and the whole lot grouped under the heading *All*. If you want to set the properties for the objects of one type, you can select that group from the drop-down list at the top of the palette.

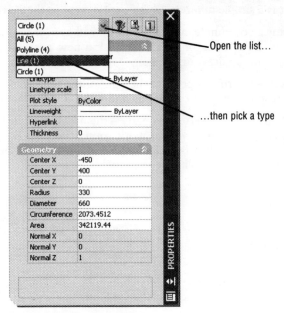

Figure 4.9 Working with multiple selections.

Auto-hide

The Properties panel is quite large, and so can get in the way. The solution is to turn on the Auto-hide function. The palette will then shrink back to a title bar when the cursor is moved away from it, and reopen when the cursor is placed over the bar.

To turn Auto-hide on or off:

1 Click on the **Properties** icon 📰 at the bottom of the palette's title bar.

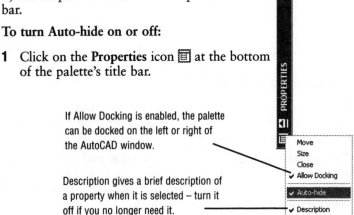

If Allow Docking is enabled, the palette can be docked on the left or right of the AutoCAD window.

Description gives a brief description of a property when it is selected – turn it off if you no longer need it.

2 The **Auto-hide** option is a toggle switch – click it to turn it on (ticked), or off.

Or

* Click the **Auto-hide** icon ▣ on the title bar – this is also a toggle switch.

Closing the palette

If the palette is not going to be wanted for a while, close it completely by clicking the Close button in the top right corner.

Exercises

1 Using the Polygon tool, draw a triangle starting at 100,100 with sides of 100 units. Set its lineweight to 0.30mm and its colour to green, by selecting from the drop-down lists.

2 Draw a square, starting at 100,0 with sides of 100 units. Change its linetype to short dashes and its colour to blue.

3 Draw a circle, centred at 150,50 with a radius of 50. Set its lineweight to 1.00mm and its colour to red.

4 Use the Offset tool to draw a second circle within the first, 25 units smaller.

5 Open the Properties palette for the triangle. Redefine its top vertex 50 units higher, making it taller.

6 Using the Properties palette, change the square's line to solid, 0.5mm and its colour to magenta.

7 Using the Properties palette, change the centre of the larger circle to 150,150.

8 Select both circles and change their colour to black, using the Properties palette.

Summary

*   You can set the type, weight and colour of lines using the drop-down lists on the Properties toolbar.

*   Lineweights can be anything from 0.0mm (hairline) up to 2.11mm.

*   There are at first only three options in the linetypes drop-down list, but more can be added easily.

*   There is a limited choice of colours on the Properties toolbar, but an unlimited choice in the Select Color dialog box.

*   The Properties palette can be used to view or change the colour, line type, position, dimensions and other properties of objects.

05 fills and hatches

In this chapter you will learn:

- how to define and apply a hatch
- how hatches can be modifed and edited
- how to define and apply a gradient fill

Hatching

Any closed shapes – rectangles, circles, ellipses, polygons and closed polylines – can be filled with a hatch pattern or texture, or with solid or shaded colour.

Shapes may have other shapes within them, creating 'islands' – and they may be nested, shapes within shapes to any number of levels. When you start the hatch routine, you pick a point within the area you want hatched. The routine then starts from the outer boundary of that area and works its way inwards. If it meets an internal boundary – i.e. a shape inside the shape – it can react in one of three ways:

* The **normal** option stops hatching at the first internal boundary, so that the first inner shape is unhatched. If it meets a further shape within this, it starts hatching again.

* The **outer** option stops hatching at the first internal boundary and leaves everything within this unhatched.

* The **ignore** option hatches everything inside the outer limits of the shape, ignoring internal boundaries.

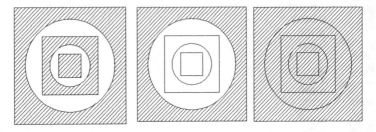

Figure 5.1 The 'island' options which apply where shapes have other shapes within them. Left to right: normal, outer and ignore.

The patterns available include ANSI and ISO standard hatches and a number of predefined ones. You can also define your own, though that is not something I have room to cover here. The patterns will normally be in the current colour (gradient fills are different), but the colour can be changed later if required.

The scales of the patterns vary, with some being much larger than others. This is not visible from the samples in the dialog box, but is immediately obvious if you try to use them at their default scale. The scale can be set in the dialog box.

To hatch a shape:

1 Click the **Hatch** button on the Draw toolbar.

2 At the **Boundary Hatch and Fill** dialog box, first select the **Pattern**. Either pick a pattern by name from the drop-down list using the **Swatch** as a guide, or...

3 Click the button to the right of the Pattern list to open the **Hatch Pattern Palette**. Switch to the **ANSI, ISO** or **Other Predefined** tab, and select a pattern. Click **OK** to return to the **Boundary Hatch and Fill** dialog box.

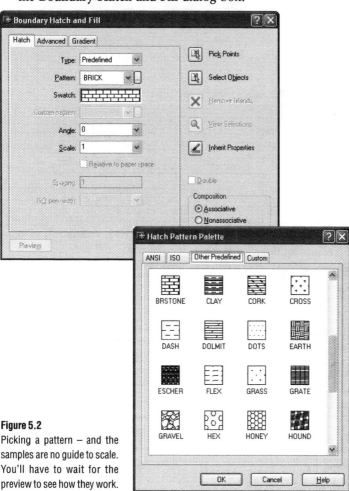

Figure 5.2

Picking a pattern – and the samples are no guide to scale. You'll have to wait for the preview to see how they work.

4 If you want to put the pattern at an angle, set the value.

5 Set the **Scale** now, or wait until after you have previewed it.

6 Go to the **Advanced** tab. Set the **Island detection style** and check that the **Island detection method** is set to *Flood*.

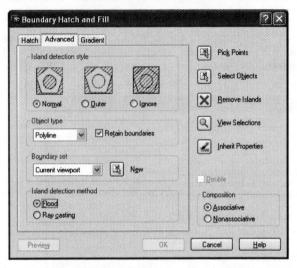

Figure 5.3 Set the island detection options on the Advanced tab. (Note that you cannot run the preview from here.)

7 Return to the **Hatch** tab and click **Pick Points** [🔩] to start selecting the area to be hatched

8 Click once inside the area to be hatched, then right-click. At the pop-up menu, select **Enter**.

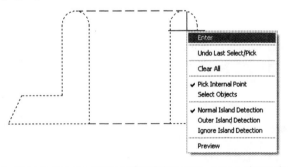

Figure 5.4 The pop-up menu during the Pick Points stage – you can change the island detection style or run a preview from here.

9 Back at the dialog box, click the **Preview** button and see how your settings work.

10 Click or press [**Escape**] to return to the dialog box to change the hatch or adjust the scale.

Or

11 Right-click to end the routine and accept the hatch.

The hatch object

The hatch does not actually fill the object, in the sense of becoming part of it. It is, in fact, a solid element with the same shape as the original, but quite separate from it. The hatch can be deleted, moved or manipulated independently of its object.

If you click on the hatched area it will be selected – its solid lines become dotted and a handle will appear at the centre.

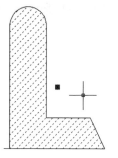

* To delete the hatch, press [**Delete**] – the original object will not be affected.

* To move the hatch, drag the handle.

* To rotate, mirror or otherwise modify the hatch, use the Modify tools as you would with any other object.

* To change the hatch colour, use the Color drop-down list in the Properties toolbar, as for lines (page 67).

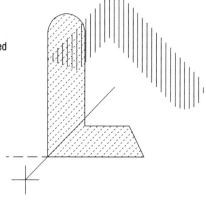

Figure 5.5 A hatch can be rotated or modified independently of its object.

The hatch may be a separate object from its shape, but it remains intimately connected. If you change the boundary of the shape, the hatch will – normally – adjust to fit the revised shape.

Hatches and layers

When a shape is hatched, selecting the hatch is simple enough, but selecting the shape itself is much trickier as the hatch overlies it. The simplest solution is to put the hatch on a different layer. You can then move down to the shape's layer and select it there if you need to modify it. Being on a different layer does not affect the connection with the shape – if its boundary is altered, the hatch's boundary will adjust to match.

Editing the hatch

The hatch pattern and its settings can also be changed. To do that, we need to get back into the Boundary Hatch dialog box.

To edit the hatch pattern:

1 Select the hatch.

2 Right-click and select **Hatch Edit...** from the pop-up menu.

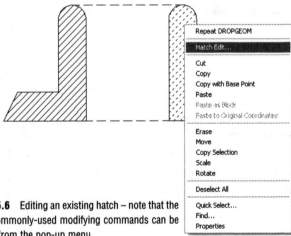

Figure 5.6 Editing an existing hatch – note that the more commonly-used modifying commands can be started from the pop-up menu.

3 The **Hatch Edit** dialog box will open.

4 Adjust the pattern, scale, size or island detection style, then click **OK**, or preview the hatch and exit from there.

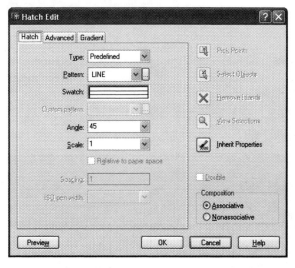

Figure 5.7 The Hatch Edit dialog box is exactly the same as the Boundary Hatch and Fill dialog box.

Gradient fills

These are applied in much the same way as hatching. The only real difference is in the way that the fill is defined.

Gradients can use one or two colours. With one colour, the fill varies from the chosen colour through to a lighter or darker version of it. With two colours, the fill varies from one to the other.

The shading can be linear or radial, with variations of each mode, and it can be set at any angle.

To fill a shape with gradient shading:

1 Click the **Hatch** button on the Draw toolbar.

2 At the **Boundary Hatch and Fill** dialog box, switch to the **Gradient** tab.

3 Select **One color,** then pick the colour and use the **Shade >
Tint** slider to set the other end of the gradient, or...

• Select **Two color** and pick the colours to use.

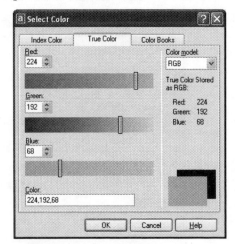

Figure 5.8 Colours are set
in the same way as for lines
(see page 71).

4 Select the style of gradient – and notice that you can fine
tune the effect by setting the **Angle,** and by turning the
Centered option on or off.

Figure 5.9 Select the style, then set the angle to adjust the effect.

5 Click **Pick Points** ⬚.

6 Click once inside the area to be hatched, then right-click. At the pop-up menu, select **Enter**.

7 Back at the dialog box, click the **Preview** button.

8 Click or press [**Escape**] to return to the dialog box to change the hatch or adjust the scale.

Or

9 Right-click to end the routine and accept the hatch.

Exercises

1 Draw a rectangle of 300 by 200, with a smaller rectangle within it. Inside this, draw four circles.

2 Using the Hatch routine, fill each of the circles with solid green or blue, then define a 45° Line hatch and apply it to the outer area and the circles. Your drawing should look like this.

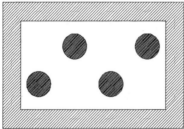

3 Delete the line hatch, then reapply it so that it only fills the outer area.

4 Using the Hatch Edit routine, apply a different hatch or gradient to all the circles.

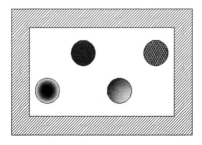

Summary

- Closed shapes can be filled with a hatch pattern or with solid or gradient colour.

- If shapes have shapes within them, the inner shapes can be hatched, or left clear, or alternate between hatched and clear.

- If a hatched object is deleted, moved or modified, its hatch is deleted moved or modified along with it. But the hatch can be deleted, moved or modified without affecting the object which it fills.

- Hatches can be redefined using the Hatch Edit routine.

- In a gradient fill, the colour shades smoothly from one to another, or making a single colour darker or lighter.

06

text and dimensions

In this chapter you will learn:

- about single line and multiline text
- how to add dimensions to lines, angles and arcs
- how to use leaders
- how to modify dimensions

Text on drawings

AutoCAD has two types of text – single and multiline. The two have much in common, but with some significant differences.

Both types of text can be used for titles, credits or annotations, and the text can be written anywhere on a drawing, and at any angle. The default size for all text is 2.5 units – and if you have changed the drawing limits significantly, this may not be suitable. Any existing text can be edited, deleted, recoloured, moved or rotated at any point. But...

♦   Single line text can only be written in the default font and cannot be formatted (apart from its colour). You cannot change the size of existing text – so check the size with the first item of text, to make sure that it is in scale with the drawing. Though you can write several lines of text at one time, so that they sit in a block, they do remain separate lines – you cannot easily rearrange the layout of text, to shorten or lengthen the lines.

♦   Multiline text can be formatted flexibly – you can apply a different font, colour, size or style to any selection of characters within a text block. The block itself can be reshaped, and the text will flow to fit the new shape.

Single line text

Single line text may have its limitations, but it can be very useful for crisp, clear annotations.

To write single line text:

1   In the Command Line, enter '*text*' to start the command.

Or

♦   Open the **Tools** menu, point to **Text** and select **Single Line Text**.

2   Pick or enter the coordinates for the start of the text.

3   You will be prompted for the height. If the current setting is suitable, press [**Enter**], otherwise enter the new value.

4   You will be prompted for the angle of rotation. Use the mouse to indicate the angle, or enter a new value, or press [**Enter**] to accept the last-used angle.

5 The I-beam cursor will appear on the drawing. Type the text, pressing **[Enter]** at the end of the line.

6 Type more lines, if required, pressing **[Enter]** after each.

7 Press **[Escape]** to end the routine.

To edit single line text:

1 Click on the text to select it, then right-click on it.

2 Select **Text Edit...** from the pop-up menu.

3 Edit the text and click **OK**.

To modify single line text:

1 Select the text.

2 Click on the appropriate tool on the Modify toolbar.

3 Move or rotate the text as you would any other object.

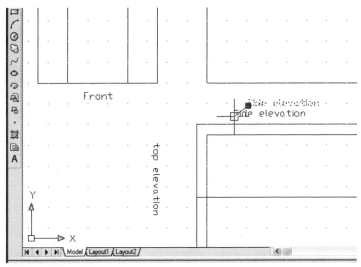

Figure 6.1 Three examples of single line text – one line was being moved when this screenshot was taken.

Wrong size text?

If your single line text is the wrong size, hard luck – you cannot change it! You will have to delete it, and rerun the Text command – setting a new size value at the start. If it is a long line, use [Ctrl]+[X] to delete the text, then [Ctrl]+[V] to paste it into the Command line when you repeat the job.

Multiline text

To write new text:

1 Click on the **Multiline Text** tool **A**.

2 Draw an outline where the text will go.

3 A text window will open and the Text Formatting toolbar will appear. Type the text as normal.

4 To format the text, select the words then use the drop-down lists and tools on the Text Formatting toolbar.

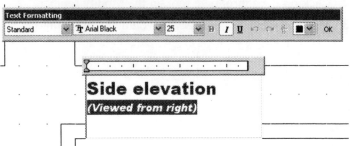

5 If the text area is too narrow, drag on the end of the ruler to widen it.

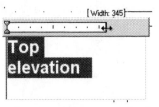

6 Click **OK** to close the text window and the formatting toolbar.

7 To edit the text or change the formatting, select and right-click on it and select **Mtext Edit...** to reopen the text window.

As an object, multiline text is more flexible than a single line. When you select the object, you will see that it has a handle at each corner – which means that you can resize it, as well as move or rotate it.

To resize the text, drag on any handle, pulling it inward or outward as required. When pulling inward, angle the movement above or below the block – it won't work if you pull directly into it.

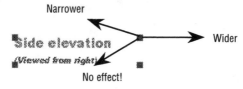

Adding dimensions

AutoCAD has a set of tools that can calculate and display the dimensions of the lines, curves and angles of your drawing. There is a different tool for each type, but all produce the dimension text and arrowed lines to show what it refers to. The size and style of the dimension text, arrows and lines can be adjusted as necessary through the Dimension Style dialog box.

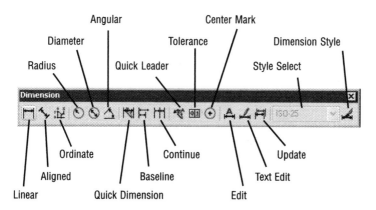

Figure 6.2 The Dimension toolbar.

Linear dimension

On horizontal and vertical lines this will give you the length. It can also be used on angled lines, but will then give the X (width) or Y (height) distance between the point at the ends of the line.

1 Click on the **Linear Dimension** tool ▦.

2 Click on one end of the line to be measured, then on the other – a new line will appear.

3 Pull the dimension line out and click when it is in clear space.

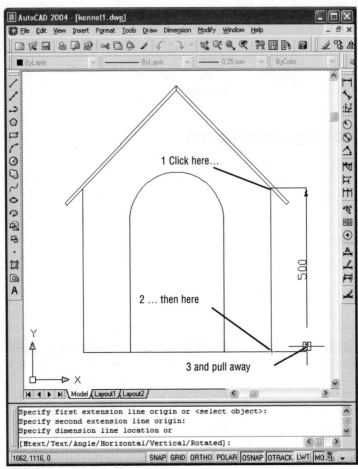

Figure 6.3 Adding a linear dimension.

Aligned dimension

This gives the length of any straight line, drawing a dimension line parallel to the one being measured. Its obvious use is with angled lines, but works equally well on horizontal or vertical ones.

1 Click on the **Aligned Dimension** tool 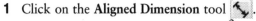.

2 Click on one end of the line to be measured, then on the other – a new line will appear.

3 Pull the dimension line outwards from the drawing and click when it is in clear space.

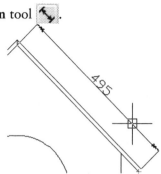

Figure 6.4 Adding an aligned dimension.

Radius and diameter dimensions

These can be used on any arc or circle, and work in the same way except for two differences. The Radius dimension line starts in the centre of the arc and the text has 'R' at the start; the diameter line runs its full width and the text is prefixed by 'Ø'.

The line can be extended beyond the arc if you want the text to be written outside.

1 Click on the **Radius** or **Diameter** **Dimension** tool.

2 Click anywhere on the arc and drag around it to set the angle of the dimension line.

3 Draw out from the arc to set the length of the line and the position of the text.

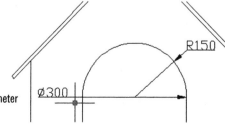

Figure 6.5 Radius and diameter dimensions.

Angular dimension

This shows the angle between two lines. These do not necessarily have to meet at a vertex.

1 Click on the **Angular Dimension** tool 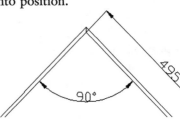.

2 Click on the first line, then on the second – a curved dimension line will appear.

3 Drag the dimension line into position.

Figure 6.6 An angular dimension.

Quick dimension

This tool allows you to set a series of linear dimensions at once, along the same dimension line.

1 Click on the **Quick Dimension** tool 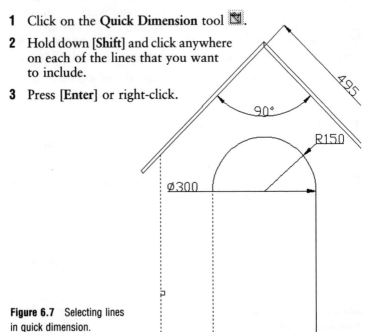.

2 Hold down [**Shift**] and click anywhere on each of the lines that you want to include.

3 Press [**Enter**] or right-click.

Figure 6.7 Selecting lines in quick dimension.

4 Drag the dimension into position.

Quick dimension gives you the
lengths of lines or the differences
between the ends of successive lines

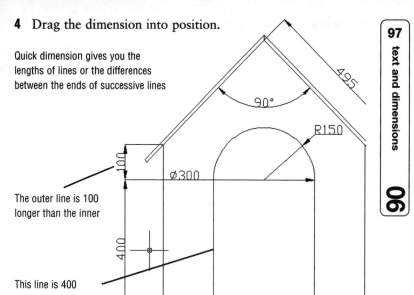

The outer line is 100
longer than the inner

This line is 400

Figure 6.8 Quick dimension.

Ordinate dimension

The Ordinate Dimension tool gives you the X or Y coordinate
of a point. This can be useful in itself, but it
can also serve as a basis for baseline dimensions (see page 98).

1 Click on the **Ordinate Dimension**
tool [icon].

2 Click on the point that you want
to label.

3 Drag the line out as required.

Figure 6.9 An ordinate dimension
– this drawing originates at Y = 0.

Baseline dimension

This produces additional dimensions from a given start, and has two distinct modes of operation.

- If you start from an ordinate dimension, it produces a series of ordinate dimensions in the same plane.

- If you start from a linear dimension, it produces extensions along the same line.

A little experimentation will help to make things clearer.

Starting from an ordinate dimension:

1 Use the **Ordinate Dimension** tool to display the X or Y co-ordinate of the point you want to use as the base.

2 Click the **Baseline Dimension** tool ▣.

3 The ordinate dimension should have been selected automatically – if it is not selected, click on it now.

4 Click on the points for which you want to add a dimension.

5 Press [**Escape**] to exit from the baseline dimension routine.

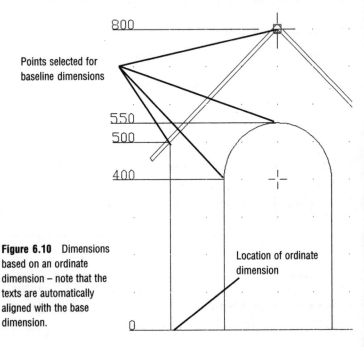

Points selected for
baseline dimensions

Figure 6.10 Dimensions based on an ordinate dimension – note that the texts are automatically aligned with the base dimension.

Location of ordinate
dimension

Starting from a linear dimension:

1 Use the **Linear Dimension** tool to show the length of the line.

2 Click the **Baseline Dimension** tool 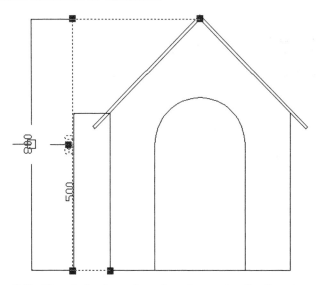.

3 Click on the end of the line which you want to use as the base.

4 Click on the points for which you want to add a dimension – the new text and lines may overlap the original dimension.

5 Press [**Escape**] to exit from the baseline dimension routine.

6 If a dimension overlaps another, click on its text to select it – the text and line will become dashed.

7 Draw the dimension text out or along into clear space, then click elsewhere to deselect it.

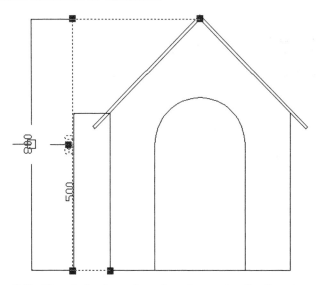

Figure 6.11 When starting from a linear dimension, new baseline dimensions are placed as extensions of the same line – which means that their texts will often overlap.

Deleting dimensions

If a dimension is no longer needed, it can be deleted – simply click anywhere on its lines or text and press [Delete]. Those created by quick dimension can be deleted individually.

Leaders

A leader is a multiline caption with an arrowed line pointing to a feature on the drawing.

1   Click on the **Quick Leader** tool 🖫.

2   Click on the object that you want to label.

3   Drag and click to create a line from the drawing.

4   If a second line is required – perhaps to angle around another object – drag and click to create it.

5   Right-click to end the line drawing part of the routine.

6   The Command Line will prompt for the text width. Type a value or right-click to accept the default.

7   You will be prompted for the text. Either type the caption into the Command Line, or right-click to open the Text window and Formatting toolbar, as for multiline text (page 92).

♦   If necessary, the caption and lines can be moved, adjusted or deleted later in the same way as any other objects.

Roofing felt

Figure 6.12   A leader with a formatted caption. The leader line always starts close to the text.

Tolerance

This places a feature control frame, to show acceptable deviations of form, position or other aspects of a feature.

The frame can be shown with or without a leader line.

To add a tolerance frame with a leader line:

1   Click on the **Quick Leader** tool 🖫.

2   The Command Line will prompt for the first leader point or [**Settings**]. Type 'S' to open the **Leader Settings** dialog box.

3   Select **Tolerance** as the **Annotation Type** and close the box.

4   Click on the object that you want to label and draw the leader.

5   Carry on as for a frame without a leader (see below).

To add a tolerance frame without a leader line:

1 Click on the **Tolerance** tool 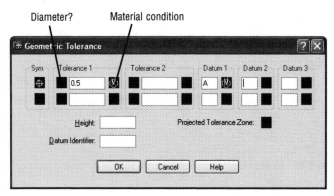 – the **Geometric Tolerance** dialog box will open.

2 Click on the **Sym** field to open the **Symbol** dialog box.

3 Select a symbol to show the type of tolerance.

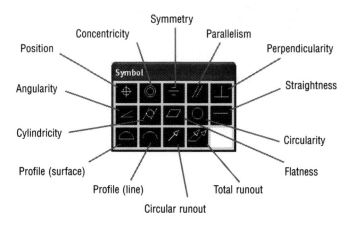

4 Enter the value for **Tolerance 1**.

5 If this applies to the diameter, click the black square on the left to show the diameter symbol (Ø).

6 If a material condition applies, click on the square to the right and select a symbol.

7 Repeat steps **4** to **6** for **Tolerance 2** if required.

8 Add one or more Datum references and complete the dialog box as required.

9 Move the new feature control frame into position.

10 If you decide that a leader line is needed, add a leader as normal, but right-click or press [**Enter**] instead of typing in text.

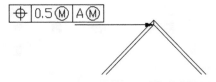

Figure 6.13 A feature control frame showing the position tolerance. This leader line was added afterwards.

Default settings

When you change the settings on things like the leader annotation type, the new setting becomes the default. Keep this in mind next time you use the tool.

Dimension style

You can control the style, size, colour and position of – and even whether or not to display – the dimension lines, arrows and text.

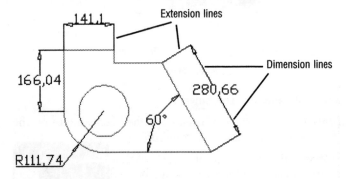

Figure 6.14 The dimension and extension lines are all optional. Text can be horizontal or aligned with its dimension.

1 Open the **Dimension** menu and select **Style...**
2 At the **Dimension Style Manager** dialog box, click **Modify**.

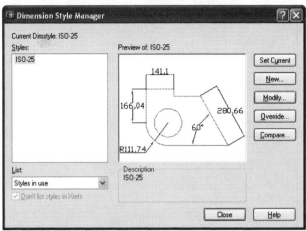

3 The **Modify Dimension Style** dialog box will open. Work through the tabs, setting the options as required (see below).

• **Lines and Arrows** controls the length and colour of dimension and extension lines, and the style and size of arrowheads. You can opt to suppress the display of any or all of the lines.

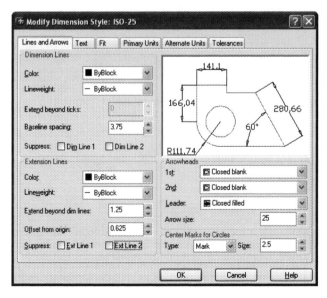

- **Text** controls the style (the font and formatting), size, colour, position and alignment of text.

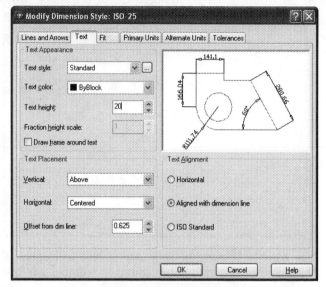

- **Fit** options specify what to do when there is not enough room for the text and arrows on dimension lines. Either can be omitted or the text can be moved beside or over the line.

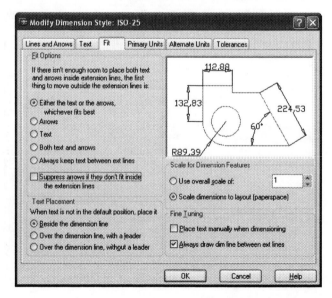

- **Primary Units** set the format and accuracy of the values for the normal linear and angular dimensions.

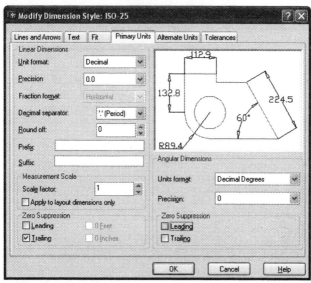

- **Alternate Units** can be displayed if required, e.g. feet and inches on a metric drawing. You can turn the display on/off and set the format and the relationship to the primary units.

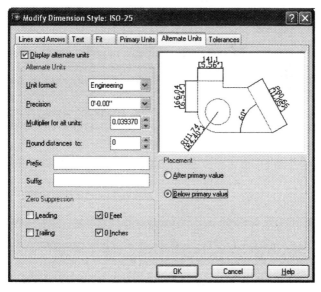

+ **Tolerances** can be also displayed, with the same or different upper and lower values.

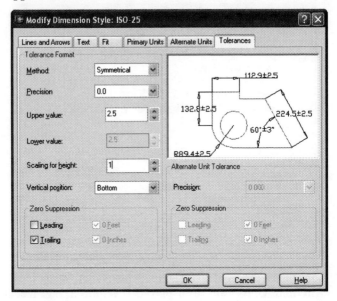

4 Click **OK** to return to the **Dimension Style Manager** dialog box, then click **Close**.

New styles

When you modify the current dimension style, the changes will be applied to all existing and any future dimensions. This may not be what you want. If you want to use different dimension styles in a drawing, you can create a new style. If this is set as the current style (in the Dimension Style Manager dialog box), existing dimensions will be unchanged. You can return to the dialog box and switch to a different style whenever it is needed.

If a style is to be used for certain types of dimensions, that can be written into its definition.

To create a style:

1 At the **Dimension Style Manager** dialog box, click **New**.

2 Give the style a name, and select which dimensions it is to be used for (if relevant).

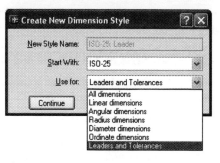

3 Click **Continue**.

4 The **New Dimension Style** dialog box is exactly the same as the **Modify** box. Work through the tabs then click **OK**.

Exercises

1 Take any existing drawing and add a title to it with single line text of a suitable size.

2 Take any existing drawing and create a simple title block, with the headings 'Title', 'Client', 'Drawn by' and 'Date'. These should be formatted in Arial. Enter 'XXX' for the text under each heading, formatting it in Courier.

3 Take any existing drawing and use the dimension tools to measure and label all the main dimensions.

4 Change the style of the new dimensions. Format the text in Times New Roman, colour the dimension and extension lines blue, and use open blank arrowheads.

5 Take any existing drawing and add leaders to identify the materials or parts of the drawing.

Summary

- AutoCAD has two types of text – single and multiline.

- Single line text cannot be formatted but is useful for quick annotations.

- Multiline text can be formatted, edited, moved or resized easily.

- The dimension tools will calculate and display the dimensions of any lines, angles or arcs, or the X or Y coordinate of a selected point.

- Leader lines and arrows can be used for labelling drawings.

- Tolerance values can be displayed.

- You can control the size, style, colour and position of dimension lines, arrows and text.

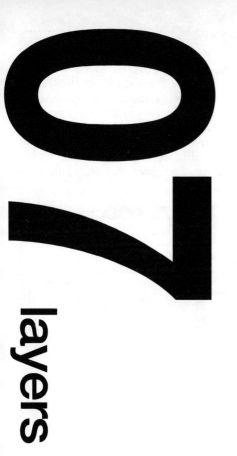

07

layers

In this chapter you will learn:

- how to make layers invisible
- about the properties of layers
- how to change an object's layer

What are layers?

Layers are the AutoCAD equivalent of overlay sheets in paper-based drawing offices. In a building drawing, for example, you might have one layer for the brickwork and woodwork, one for the wiring, one for the plumbing, and so on. As layers can be hidden, you can display or print any single layer or combination of layers, to give an uncluttered view of selected features. You can assign a colour, linetype and lineweight to a layer, which helps to identify sets of features and gives consistency to their appearance.

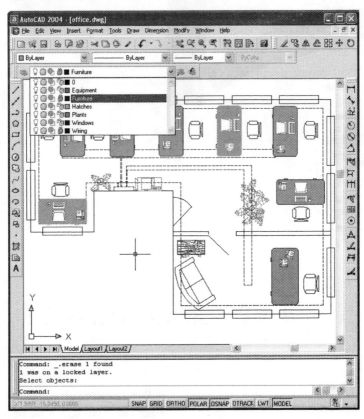

Figure 7.1 In this office drawing, the walls, windows, wiring, furniture, equipment, hatches and plants are all on separate layers. The drop-down list on the Layers toolbar can be used for changing between layers and setting their properties.

The Layers toolbar

At the centre of the Layers toolbar is the drop-down list where you can see and control the key properties of layers.

◆ **Freezing** makes layers invisible, but also has a deeper impact. When a layer is frozen, AutoCAD completely ignores it when regenerating and redrawing a model. **Thaw** the layer to bring it back into active use. A layer can be frozen in the current viewport only, or in all viewports. (See page 140 to find out about viewports.)

◆ **On/off** simply toggles the visibility of a layer. When turned off, a layer is not displayed or plotted. Freeze layers that are not likely to be needed for a while; use On/off to hide layers on a temporary basis.

◆ **Lock** prevents objects on a layer from being edited or deleted.

◆ **Colour** shows the default colour for lines and hatches on the layer. You cannot change the colour from here.

To change properties using the toolbar:

1 Click on any of the property icons, the layer name or the drop-down arrow on the right to open the list.

2 Click on the layer name to switch to a different layer.

3 Click on the icon to toggle between on/off, freeze/thaw or lock/unlock. You cannot freeze a layer while it is current – if necessary switch to another layer first.

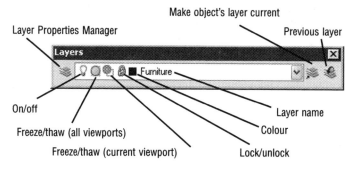

Figure 7.2 The Layers toolbar. To make an object's layer current, first select the object, then click the toolbar button.

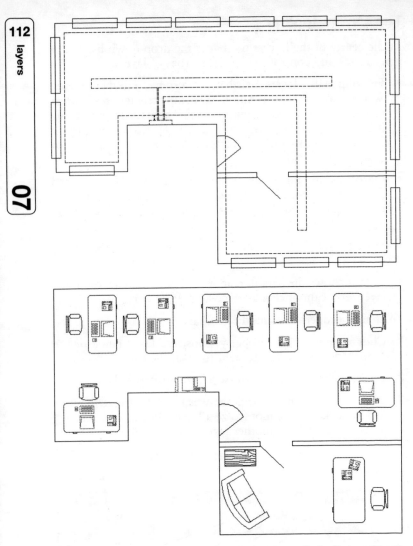

Figure 7.3 Two views of the same drawing. In the top one, the furniture, equipment, hatches and plants layers have been turned off so that the structural features can be seen more clearly. In the bottom view, the structural features have been hidden so that the layout of furniture and equipment is more obvious.

Creating layers

When you start a new drawing, it has only one layer, 'Layer 0'. New layers can be created at any stage. As objects can be moved from one layer to another, you can create a layer before drawing the objects on it, or afterwards.

Layer 0 has the default settings for colour (white – or black if the background is white), linetype and lineweight. When a layer is created, it will have the same settings as whichever existing layer is selected at the time, or the default settings if no layer is selected.

Layers are created in the **Layer Properties Manager** dialog box. This has a small set of tools for managing layers, and displays the full range of layer properties. These include Linetype, Lineweight, Plot style and Plot (on/off) which are not shown on the Layers toolbar – you may need to scroll the display across to see the properties on the far right of the set.

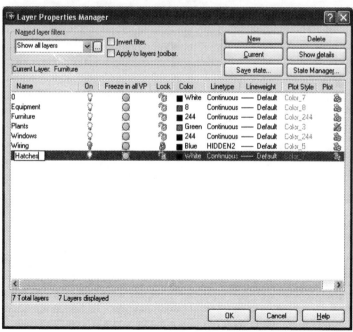

Figure 7.4 The **Layer Properties Manager** dialog box. The width of the columns can be adjusted by dragging on the dividing lines in the header row. Here, as the names are all short, the Name column has been shrunk to bring the rest into view.

To create a new layer:

1 Open the **Format** menu and select **Layer…**

Or

+ Click the **Layer Properties Manager** tool on the **Layers** toolbar.

2 If you want the layer to start with the same settings as an existing one, select it now, otherwise click in the blank area of the window so that no layer is selected.

3 Click **New**.

4 A new layer will be listed. Replace the default name '*Layer1*' (or whatever number) with a more meaningful name.

5 Set the layer's properties – see page 115.

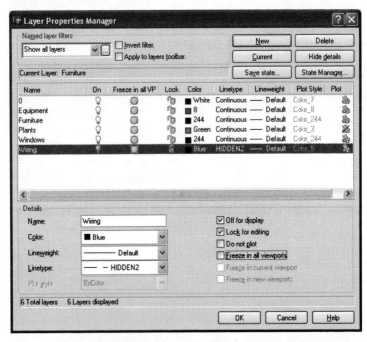

Figure 7.5 The Layer Properties Manager dialog box, with the Details displayed at the bottom. The filters, at the top left of the box, allow you to list only those layers that meet certain criteria. There isn't room in this small book to cover filters, but if you have a lot of layers, you should explore them.

To set layer properties:

1 If you want the full Details display, click the **Show details** button – and click **Hide details** when they are no longer wanted.

2 With the toggles (on/off) – **On, Freeze, Lock** and **Plot** – click on the icon or the checkbox in the Details area to switch from one state to the other.

3 To set the **Colour, Linetype** or **Lineweight**, click on the icon to open the related dialog box, or open the drop-down lists in the **Details** area to select an option there.

4 To change the name, double-click on the name in the main list, or click into the **Name** field in the Details area. Edit as with any other text.

5 Click **OK** to close the **Layer Properties Manager** dialog box when you have finished.

To delete a layer:

1 If there are any objects on the layer, delete them, or move them to other layers (see below).

2 Open the **Layer Properties Manager** dialog box.

3 Select the layer.

4 Click **Delete**.

Objects and layers

New objects are always created in the current layer, whatever that may be. An organized person will set the layer, then create the objects for it. Not all of us are that organized, and when we are focused on what we are drawing, we may lose sight of where we are drawing it. It is also all too easy to be mistaken about what layer is current – if an object is selected, its layer is displayed on the Layers toolbar.

To move objects between layers:

1 Select the object.

2 Drop down the **Layers** list.

3 Click on the layer that you want to move the object onto.

Sometimes, this doesn't work and the object will stay resolutely on the same layer despite you best efforts! There is a solution.

To move objects between layers using the Properties:

1 Select the object.

2 Right-click and select **Properties** from the pop-up menu.

3 Open the **Layer** drop-down list and select the new layer from there.

4 Close the **Properties** palette if it is no longer wanted.

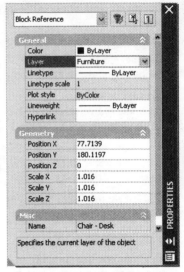

Exercises

1 Create a simple drawing or open an existing one and add extra details, text, dimensions and hatches, placing these on different layers.

2 Give each layer a different colour, and change the linestyle and weight on the dimensions layer to make its lines more distinctive.

3 Look back at other existing drawings and see if the use of layers would make them more manageable.

Summary

- ◆ Layers are like overlay sheets in drawings on paper. They can be turned on or off, or locked to prevent changes.

- ◆ You can see and control the key properties of layers from the Layers toolbar.

- ◆ New layers are created in the Layer Properties Manager dialog box.

- ◆ You can move an object from one layer to another.

08

blocks and the designcenter

In this chapter you will learn:

- how a set of objects can be made into a block
- how to insert blocks in to drawings
- about the DesignCenter and DC online

Blocks

A block is a set of objects that can be handled as a single unit, and which is identifed by name. If you have several instances of the same component in a drawing, you could draw it once, convert that to a block, then insert copies of the block as required.

The larger and more complex the drawing, the more useful you will find blocks. It is much simpler to insert a named block than to select a set of objects, especially if those objects are close to or overlap others which are not part of the set.

Making blocks

First double-check the objects that are to be converted into a block. Make sure that everything is in place and that if any formatting (see Chapter 4) is required, it has been done. You can edit blocks, but it is far simpler to get it right in the first place.

To make a block:

1 Select the objects.

2 Click the **Make Block** tool 🔳 on the Draw toolbar.

3 At the **Block Definition** dialog box, enter a **Name** to identify the block.

4 Click the **Pick point** button 🔳 then pick a point on or near the objects to act as a base point. This will be used for locating the block when it is inserted or moved.

Or

• Type the coordinates of the base point.

5 If you need to add to or change the set of objects, click 🔳 to select them.

6 In the **Preview icon** area, click **Create icon from block geometry** if you want to give the block a preview. This can be useful when selecting blocks for inserting.

7 Type a **Description** if it might be useful in the future.

8 Leave the other settings at their defaults and click **OK**.

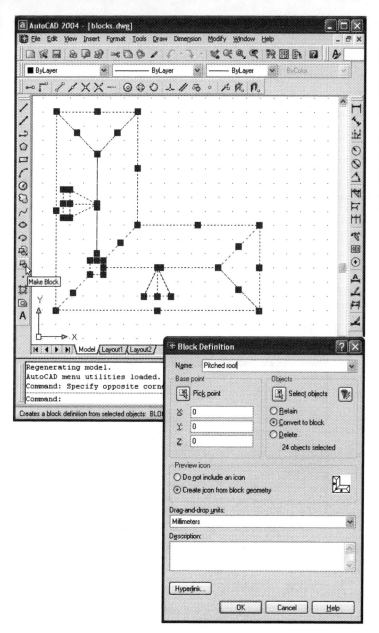

Figure 8.1 Making a block. The objects can then be copied or moved as a single unit.

Inserting blocks

If you can see the block in your working area, you can copy it with the usual techniques. If it is not visible, you can locate it by name using the Insert Block routine.

You can set the position, scale and rotation by typing the values into the dialog box or by manipulating the block on screen.

1 Click the **Insert Block** tool on the Draw toolbar.

2 Select the block from the **Name** drop-down list.

3 For the **Insertion point**, tick the **Specify On-screen** checkbox or enter the X, Y (and Z if in 3D) coordinates.

4 To set the **Scale** factor, tick the **Specify On-screen** checkbox or enter the X, Y (and Z) values.

5 To set a **Rotation**, tick the **Specify On-screen** checkbox or enter the angle.

6 If you want to be able to edit the components of the block after placing it, tick the **Explode** checkbox.

7 Click **OK**.

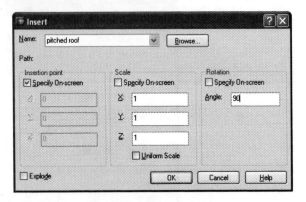

Figure 8.2   Insert a block. Only the Insertion point is essential.

Inserting drawings

A complete drawing can be inserted into another. Use the Insert Block tool to start, then Browse for the drawing file at the Insert dialog box, and insert it as if it were a block.

Editing blocks

A block is a single unit. If you need to change any of its component lines or shapes you can explode it, but – as we saw earlier – you cannot unexplode something. If you want it back into a block after editing, you will have to use the Make Block routine again. A better solution is to edit it.

1 Right-click on the block and select **Edit Block in-place** from the pop-up menu.

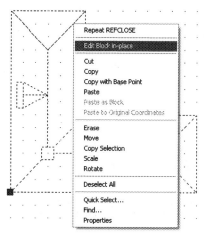

Or

• Open the **Modify** menu, point to **Xref and Block Editing** and select **Edit Reference In-Place,** then click on the block.

2 At the **Reference Edit** dialog box click **OK**.

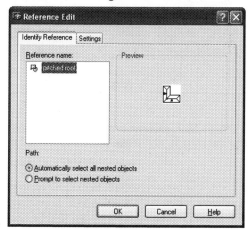

The **Refedit** toolbar will appear.

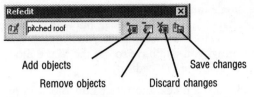

Add objects

Remove objects

Save changes

Discard changes

3 To edit a component line or shape, select it and move or modify using the normal tools.

4 To remove a component from the block, select it and click **Remove objects from working set** .

5 To add a new component to the block, select it and click **Add objects to working set** .

6 When you have finished, click **Save changes** or **Discard changes** to revert to the design before editing.

◆ Simply closing the **Refedit** toolbar does not end the editing routine. You must save or discard the changes to end.

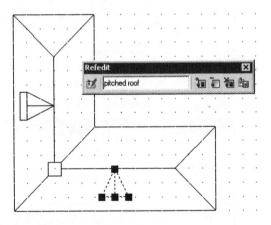

Figure 8.3 Editing a block. The selected component can now be moved, modified or removed without affecting the other components.

The DesignCenter

The DesignCenter gives you easy access to the blocks and other features of the drawing files on your system – including the very many objects in the sample files that are supplied with AutoCAD. It can also be used to access the huge range of predefined blocks at DC online (AutoDesk's web site).

To display the DesignCenter:

1 Open the **Tools** menu and select **DesignCenter**.

Or

Press [**Control**] + [**2**].

The DesignCenter, like the Properties palette, can float anywhere on the screen or be docked to the left or right of the working area.

Toggles:

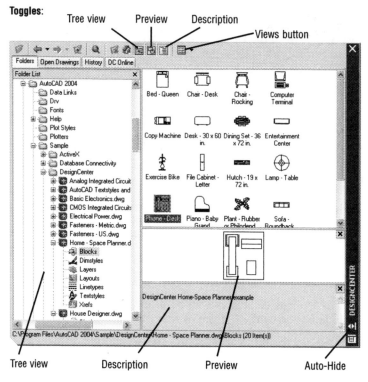

Figure 8.4 The DesignCenter – and I don't know why AutoCAD insists on spelling it as a single word!

It has four panes – three of which can be toggled on and off:

- **Tree view** shows the folders, which can be opened to show the drawings, which can be opened to show their blocks and other elements.

- **Preview** gives you a close-up of the selected block.

- **Description** gives the specification or a brief description of the selected block.

The main pane shows the contents of the selected folder or drawing. As in My Computer in Windows, the contents can be viewed as small or large icons, a list or 'details' (which actually has no details at all!). Large icons are probably the most useful.

Inserting a block

Inserting a block is straightforward – at the simplest you can just drag it from the DesignCenter onto the drawing. The tricky bit is getting the scale right, as the drawing that the block is coming from and the one that it is going into may have quite different scales. For example, if you drop in a block from the *House Designer* sample drawing into one started with the default settings, it will be so big that you may have to zoom out to be able to see it!

The solutions are not difficult – you just have to remember that you may need to use them.

To insert a block with drag and drop:

1 In the DesignCenter, open the folders to reach the drawing, then open the drawing to get the list of elements, and finally select the *Blocks* heading to display the blocks.

2 Select the block and drag it onto the drawing.

3 Release the mouse to drop it onto the drawing.

4 The DesignCenter may well be in the way – click the **Auto-hide** button at the bottom of the title bar.

5 Click on the block to select it. You should see a single blue handle on or near it. Drag on this handle to move the block.

6 If the block is the wrong size, use the **Scale** tool (page 56). You may find it simpler to type a scale factor, rather than use the mouse, especially if you want to make the block smaller.

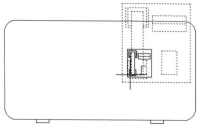

Figure 8.5 Blocks inserted from other drawings may well need to be scaled to suit your drawing.

To insert a block with the Insert dialog box:

1 In the DesignCenter, select the blocks.

2 Right-click on it and select **Insert Block...**

Or

♦ Open the **Insert** menu and select **Block...**

3 Complete the **Insert** dialog box as if you were inserting a block from the same drawing (see page 120).

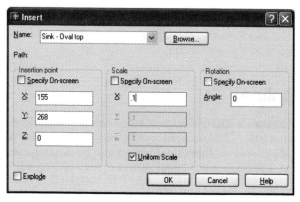

Scale and units

If you going to bring a number of blocks in from other drawings, and they are all or most at the same scale, you can set the default scale factor in the Drawing Units dialog box. If you will be using samples from the DesignCenter in a standard metric drawing, you should find that they fit better if you set the scale to *Centimeters* instead of the default *Millimeters*.

To set the default scale:

1 Open the **Format** menu and select **Units…**

2 In the **Drag-and-drop scale** area, drop down the **Units** list and select an appropriate unit.

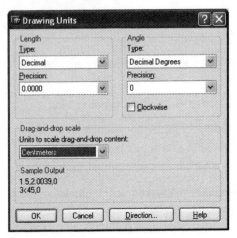

3 Click **OK**.

4 Insert a block to test the effect, and try a different unit if it comes in at the wrong scale.

DC Online

AutoCAD runs a DesignCenter Online service, offering a wide selection of 2D and 3D blocks, produced by its own people and by outside suppliers. Individual blocks can be downloaded free of charge, or you can buy them in sets at very reasonable rates.

To insert blocks from DC Online:

1 In the DesignCenter, switch to the **DC Online** tab.

2 If you are not already online, you will need to connect to the Internet at this point.

3 Wait for the Category Listing to download. It will appear as a folder display in the left-hand frame and as a simpler listing in the top pane.

4 Open the folders to reach those that contain blocks – these are normally at the third level down.

5 Click on an icon in the contents display to see its preview and details in the lower pane.

6 To capture the block, click the **Save this symbol as...** link and save it as a drawing file on your system.

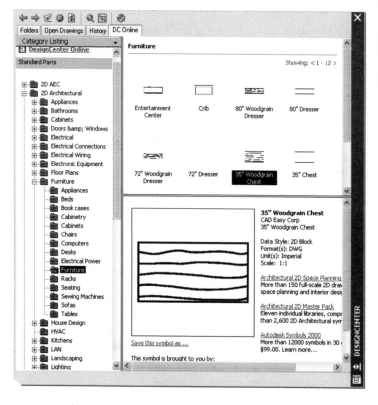

• The saved block can be inserted through the DesignCenter, using the Tree view display to locate the drawing's folder; or through the Insert Block routine (see page 120), using the **Browse** button to locate the file.

Exercises

1 We are going to make a spiral staircase.

Draw a circle of 10 unit radius at 100,100.

Draw a polyline using these coordinates: 100,100; 30,100; 39,145; 100,100. Use the Trim tool to remove the ends of the polyline within the circle.

Copy the polyline using a polar array, centring it at 100,100 and making 10 copies over an angle of –270°.

Make the drawing into a block, naming it 'spiral'.

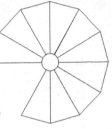

2 Insert the spiral block into another drawing, adjusting its scale to suit, and rotating it as necessary.

3 Explore DC Online, downloading at least 2 blocks and inserting them into your drawings.

Summary

- A set of lines and shapes can be made into a block, for easier handling and copying.

- When inserting a block into a drawing, you can set its position, scale and angle.

- A block can be exploded into its component parts.

- The DesignCenter gives you easy access to the blocks on your system and at DC online.

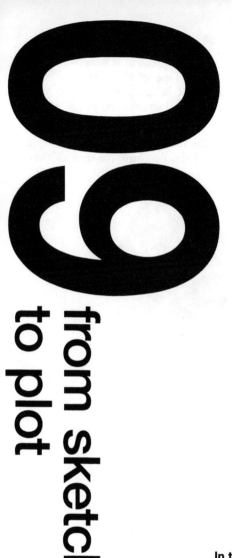

09 from sketch to plot

In this chapter you will learn:

- about plans and elevations
- about plotters, paper sizes and scaled output
- how to set up layouts
- about viewports
- how to preview and plot

Sketches

All drawings start in the head. The question is how best to get them from there into AutoCAD. One of the best methods is through sketches. They need not be accurate – that's what AutoCAD is there for – but they will enable you to get an idea into a workable shape.

The first stage is to translate the idea (Figure 9.1) into a rough sketch (Figure 9.2). This should should show the overall shape and dimensions.

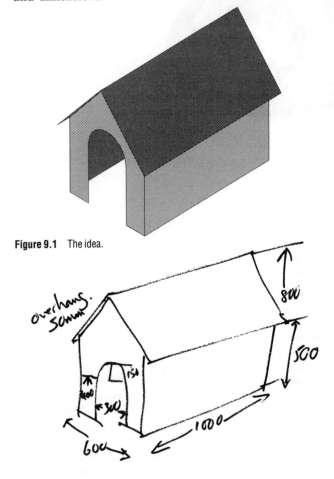

Figure 9.1 The idea.

Figure 9.2 The first sketch.

Orthographic projection

Though AutoCAD can display models in 3D, the majority of technnical drawings are still 2D, and normally use *orthographic projection*. This shows the object from the top (the plan), the end or side (side elevation) and the front (front elevation).

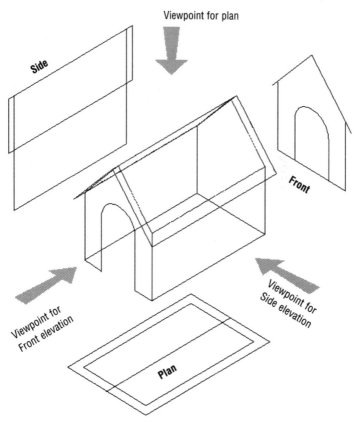

Figure 9.3 Orthographic projection – how the plan, front and side drawings relate to the object.

If we apply the orthographic principles to our 3D sketch, we can derive these sketches:

* **The plan** – a top-down view of the object, showing the widths and lengths of its components (Figure 9.4).

* **The front elevation** – how the object looks when seen flat-on

from the front. This should be marked with the widths and heights of its parts (Figure 9.5).

- **The side elevation** – how the object looks from the side (left or right). Lengths and heights should be on here (Figure 9.6).

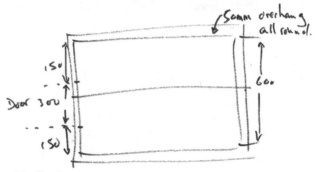

Figure 9.4 The plan.

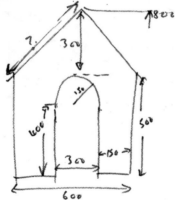

Figure 9.5 The front elevation.

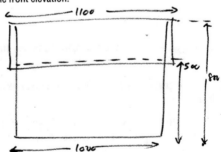

Figure 9.6 The side elevation.

- You may also need one or more **sections** through the object if there are features inside that cannot be seen from the front or side.

The sketches do not have to be complete. In the example here, the width of the sloping roof is not known. It could be calculated, but there is no point in spending time doing this as AutoCAD can work out dimensions for you.

Model space and paper output

So far, we have only been working on screen, so we have only had to think about the size of the model space. In the working world, plans are normally printed out onto paper and drawn to certain standard scales, such as 1:10 or 1:200. This means that we have to think about paper sizes and drawing scale when setting up the model space.

The first question is 'What size is model space?' What are the outside dimensions of the object, or if your drawing is of the plan, front and side elevations, what is the total length and width of the space that they would be laid out in? Once again, a paper sketch helps – all you need is a rough sketch with the main dimensions.

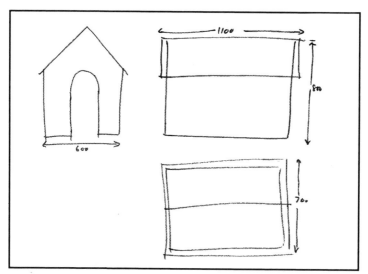

Figure 9.7 A sketch of the layout, with the outside dimensions.

In the example in Figure 9.7, the model space must be at least 600 + 1100 long, and 800 + 700 wide. Allowing an extra 200 each way for dimension text, the model space needs to be at least 1900 by 1700.

I'm using millimetres, but AutoCAD can work in any unit. The commonly used drawing units are *Architectural* (feet and inches with fractions), *Engineering* (feet and inches with decimal fractions) and *Decimal*, which is normally used with metric units but you can have any unit at all – feet, cubits or whatever. The type of unit, and how they are displayed does not really become important until you start to add dimensions. At the setup stage it is enough to work out the size of your model space in whole units.

Paper sizes

There are three sets of paper sizes in common use: ISO, ANSI and Architectural. The sets are very similar, with the largest size around 900 × 1200mm (33 × 44"), and four smaller sizes, each half the size of the one before. (Architectural has an extra intermediate size.)

	ISO		ANSI		Architectural
A0	841 × 1189mm	E	34 × 44"	Large E	36 × 48"
				E	30 × 42"
A1	594 × 841mm	D	22 × 34"	D	24 × 36"
A2	420 × 594mm	C	17 × 22"	C	18 × 24"
A3	297 × 420mm	B	11 × 17"	B	12 × 18"
A4	210 × 297mm	A	8½ × 11"	A	9 × 12"

What size of paper will the drawing be printed on?

Printers and plotters rarely work right up to the edge of the sheet. What is the actual size available for your drawing? If you don't know, you can find out when you first start to plot a drawing, as AutoCAD will tell you the plottable area of the sheet.

Standard scales

You can use any scale you like for your drawing – AutoCAD will happily work with any scale value – but the working world tends to use certain scales. These are nice round numbers if you are working in metres, less so for feet and inches.

Typical use	Scale	Scale factor
Area plans	1 = 200mm	200
Building plans	1 = 100mm	100
House plans	1 = 50mm	50
Details	1 = 20mm	20
Fine details	1 = 10mm	10
Area plans	$^1/_{16}$" = 1'	192
Building plans	$^1/_8$" = 1'	96
House plans	$^1/_4$" = 1'	48
Details	$^1/_2$" = 1'	24
Fine details	1" = 1'	12

Calculating the scale

Time to get the calculator out! You need to divide the length and breadth of the minimum model space by those of your paper. It doesn't have to be a very accurate result, because you are then going to take the highest of the two values and round this up to the nearest standard scale.

For example, my dog kennel drawing needs a minimum model space of 1900 by 1700, I am plotting on A4 paper and the plotter leaves a margin of 7mm all round. The plottable size is therefore 283 × 196.

Length scale = 1900 / 283 = 6.7

Width scale = 1700 / 196 = 8.7

Largest scale = 8.7

Next standard scale = 10

If you now multiply the usable paper size by the scale, you will get the maximum available model space – in this case, 2830 × 1960. If you set your drawing limits to this, you will have a clear correlation between the model space and the paper size.

Let's look at an example in imperial measures. We are drawing house plans with an overall size of 45 × 38', the paper is Architectural D (24 × 36") but with a ½" margin all round.

As the plans are in feet and the paper size is in inches, we must convert the plan lengths to inches.

Length scale = (45 × 12) / 35 = 15.4

Width scale = (38 × 12) / 23 = 19.8

Largest scale = 19.8

Next standard scale = 24 = ½" = 1'

Multiplying the paper size by the scale (and dividing by 12 to give the results in feet), we find that we can draw plans up to 70 × 46' on Architectural D paper at ½" = 1'.

Know your limits

If you regularly use the same size of paper, it will be worth spending a few minutes working out the maximum drawing limits at the standard scales for that paper.

Setting up and drawing

Once you have worked out the size of your model space, you can set up a file for the drawing.

1 Use **File > New** and select the **Start from scratch** option. Set the Default settings to Metric or Imperial as required.

2 Set the drawing units and drawing limits to suit your plan and the model space – see pages 8 to 10 if you have forgotten how.

3 Turn on the grid, and the snap, if required, and start drawing!

♦ While you are simply drawing in model space, you don't have to think about scale or the paper output – just keep within your drawing limits.

4 When you start to add dimensions and/or text, scale matters again. Adjust the size of the text and arrows to suit your scale (see Chapter 6).

You can print directly from model space, but if you want properly scaled and professionally presented output, you should use layouts.

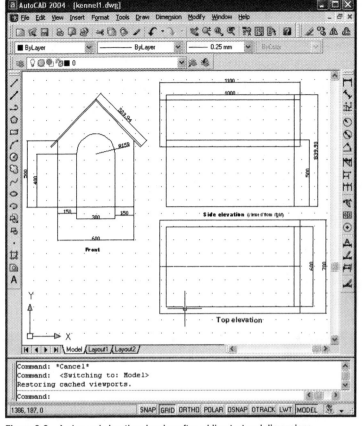

Figure 9.8 A plan and elevation drawing after adding text and dimensions.

Layouts

A layout is a view of model space, perhaps with annotations or other enhancements, prepared for output to a plotter or printer. It can show the whole of the drawing or just a part of it. It can include text, dimensions and additional drawn items that are not present in model space. For instance, you would normally place the title block on a layout, rather than in model space where it would just be clutter.

Each layout is designed for a specific plotter/printer and paper size, and displays the drawing in a specific view. It is possible to change the plotter, paper and view later, but any changes may affect the way that the material fits onto the layout. Unless there is a good reason for changing, it is probably better to set up a new layout with the required settings.

To create a layout from scratch:

1 Click on a layout tab. The **Page Setup** dialog box will appear.

◆ There are two layout tabs when you start. If you need more, right-click on any tab and select **New layout**.

2 Go to the **Plot Device** tab and select the plotter or printer. The rest of this tab can be safely left at the defaults.

3 Switch to the **Layout Settings** tab.

4 Select the **Paper size** – and notice the **Printable area** figures, if this is the first time that you have used it.

5 Set the orientation as required.

6 The **Plot scale** can be set to *Scaled to fit*, to maximize the use of the paper, or to the design scale of the drawing.

7 Click **OK** to close the dialog box and see the layout.

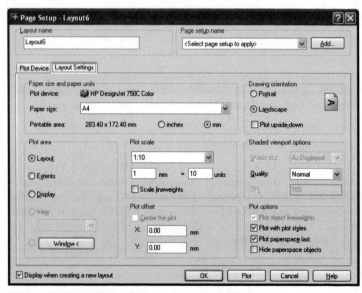

Figure 9.9 Always check – and set – the Plot Device first.

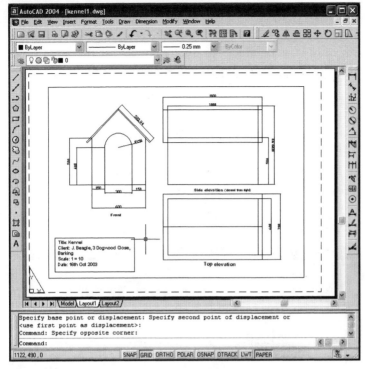

Figure 9.10 A simple layout with a title block.

You can now add a title block, annotations or even more drawn objects. These will only be present on the layout – go back to the model space, and you will find that the drawing is untouched.

Accessing model space

It is possible to go into model space through a layout – double-click on drawing area to go in, and outside the drawing area to return to the layout level. Use this to adjust the view of the drawing – once you are in model space you can zoom and pan over the drawing to bring a part into focus. You can also draw or add notes while you are there, but if you are not careful you will add items to model space that are only wanted on the layout. If you want to add to the drawing, go to the Model tab and do it there.

Viewports

A viewport divides the screen into two or more areas so that you can look at your model in different ways at the same time. Viewports can be created in model space and in layouts – the technique is the same in both.

The screen can be divided into up to four viewports. Any or all of the resulting viewports can then be further divided likewise. You also have a set of predefined viewports to choose from, and can create your own.

To divide the screen:

1   Open the **View** menu, point to **Viewports** and select **1, 2, 3** or **4 viewports**.

2   You may be asked to choose **Horizontal** or **Vertical** division.

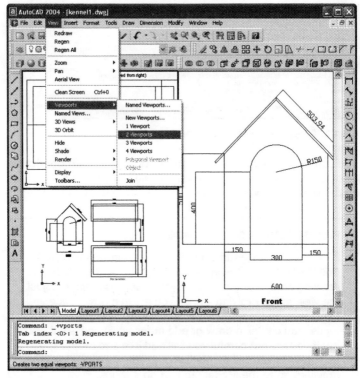

Figure 9.11   This screen was first divided vertically into two viewports, then the left side was selected and divided again.

3 If required, click into a viewport to be subdivided and repeat the steps.

Or

4 Open the **View** menu, point to **Viewports** and select **New Viewports...**

5 The **Viewports** dialog box will open with the **New Viewports** tab at the front.

6 Click on the name of a viewport to see a preview of the screen division.

7 When you find a suitable layout, click **OK**.

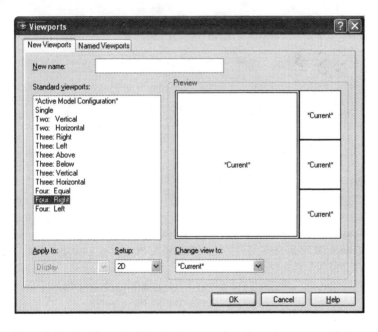

Figure 9.12 The Viewports dialog box. If you create a viewport arrangement that you may want to reuse, go to the **New Viewports** tab, select "Active Model Configuration" and give it a new name. This will then be stored on the **Named Viewports** tab.

Plotters and plotting

The plotters and printers installed in Windows are available in AutoCAD, but for best results (see the boxed item below), you should install them in AutoCAD through the Plotter Manager.

1 In the **Tools** menu, point to **Wizards** and select **Add Plotter...**

2 Work through the wizard – it is almost identical to the printer wizard in Windows.

3 At the Plotter Model stage, select from the lists of **Manufacturers** and **Models**, or click **Have Disk...** to use the installation disk supplied with the device.

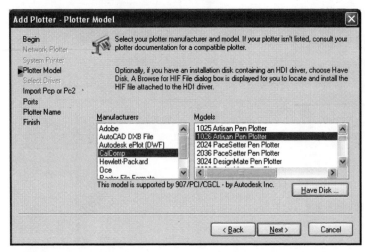

Figure 9.13 If your device is not on the list and you do not have a disk for it, you can still use it if it is installed at Windows level.

4 Carry on through the wizard – you will probably find it useful to run the calibration routine at the end.

Problems of scale

In theory, if you have set up your model space and pages properly, the drawing that you have set to 1 = 10, or whatever scale, should be plotted (or printed) to that scale. However, if you are using a Windows plotter/printer driver, rather than an AutoCAD one, the output may not be exactly to scale.

Preview and plot

When you have finished adding to the layout, you can plot it directly, or check the preview first – this is worth doing, even though the layout gives a very good idea of the plotted output.

1 Right-click on the layout's tab and select **Plot...** to open the **Plot** dialog box. This is almost identical to that for the **Page Setup,** but with one significant difference. At the bottom left you will see two preview buttons.

2 Click a preview button. Click:

Full Preview... to see the layout as it will look when plotted.

Partial Preview... to get a dialog box that tells you the paper size and printable area, and warns you of any problems.

3 Press [**Escape**] to exit the full preview.

Or

♦ Click **OK** to close the **Partial Preview** dialog box.

4 Click **OK** to send the layout to the plotter.

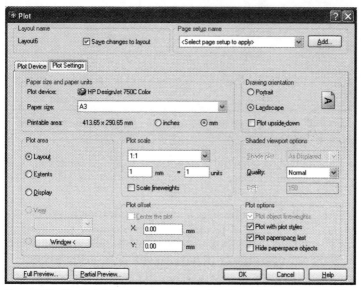

Figure 9.14 The Plot dialog box. If you look back to Figure 9.9 you will see that the Page Setup dialog box has a Plot button, so that you can also plot from there.

The Layout Wizard

The wizard offers a quick way to set up a layout, and provides the simplest way to get a ready-made title block into a drawing.

1 In the **Tools** menu, point to **Wizards** and then select **Create Layout...**

2 The first few steps cover the **Printer**, **Paper Size** and **Orientation** – make your selections as usual.

3 At the **Title Block** step, if you want to use one, select a ready-made block suitable for your paper size and orientation.

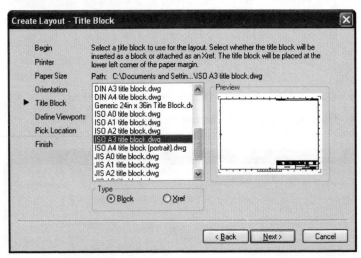

Figure 9.15 The ready-made title blocks save time, though there is only a limited choice for each paper size.

4 At the **Define Viewports** step, select **Single** to use the current view in model space – the other options are for 3D drawings and other more advanced work.

5 At the **Pick Location** step, click **Select Location** to go into the layout and draw a rectangle where you want the drawing. The wizard dialog box disappears while you are doing this. Take the opportunity to have a good look at the layout.

6 If you are not happy with the title block, use the **Back** button to work back to the Title Block step and reselect.

Figure 9.16 Defining the location for the drawing area.

7 Click **Finish**.

8 To edit the title block, double-click on it. The **Enhanced Attribute Editor** dialog box will open.

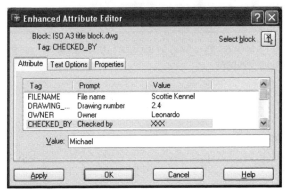

Figure 9.17 Editing the title block values.

9 Work through the tags, clicking on each in turn and typing your details in as the Value. Click **OK** when you have done.

10 If you want to move the drawing area on the layout, click and drag on its border to move the area.

11 If you want to resize the drawing area, click on its border then drag on a handle to make the area larger or smaller.

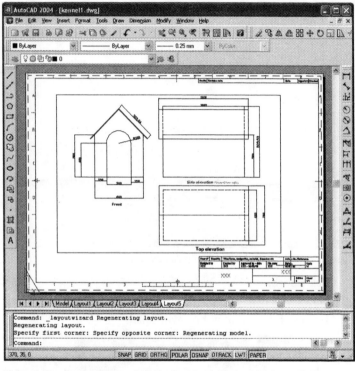

Figure 9.18 A new layout produced by the wizard. The next job is to edit the attributes in the title block.

Exercises

1   Take an existing drawing, go to its layout tab and send it to your plotter using the default settings. Examine the result.

2   Find out what you can about the plotters and printers which you can use. What paper sizes can they handle. What are their printing areas.

3   Use the Layout Wizard to set up a drawing for a selected plotter. Include a template and edit the attributes in the title block.

Summary

*   It often helps to start by sketching your ideas on paper.

*   The majority of technnical drawings are 2D, and use orthographic projection.

*   If you want to plot to a standard scale, you have to think about paper sizes and drawing scale when setting up the model space.

*   There are three sets of paper sizes in common use: ISO, ANSI and Architectural.

*   A layout is view of model space, prepared for output to a plotter.

*   A viewport divides the screen into two or more areas.

*   Plotters and printers should be installed in AutoCAD, using the Plotter Manager.

*   You can preview a layout before sending it to the plotter.

*   The Layout Wizard offers a quick way to set up a layout, especially if you want to add a title block.

10

drawing in 3D

In this chapter you will learn:

- about 3D drawing modes
- the Z coordinate and the X, Y, Z axes
- how to draw wireframes in 3D
- about 3D views and 3D orbit
- how to plot 3D drawings

3D modes

AutoCAD has three different 3D drawing modes, and you cannot easily switch objects from one mode to another. In practice, you need to decide which mode is appropriate for the job and use that. The modes are:

- **Wireframe** is an extension of standard 2D drawing into the third dimension. Objects are defined and displayed in terms of edges and points, but have no surfaces. Wireframe drawing is very time-consuming, but at least it uses the same tools and techniques as 2D work. We will use the rest of this chapter to look at wireframes.

- **Surface** drawing defines objects in terms of their faces using a polygonal mesh. As each unit of the mesh is flat, rounded surfaces are not truly curved. Surface models are about as time-consuming as wireframes to construct, and are created with the special Surface tools and techniques. There simply is not enough space in this book to cover these.

- **Solid** models are built up from a set of basic 3D shapes – box, wedge, cylinder, sphere, cone and torus (or donut). These can be adapted and combined to construct any other shape. Of the three modes, solids are the simplest to use and we shall look at them in Chapter 11.

The Z coordinate

In AutoCAD, the X, Y, Z coordinate system is screen-based – not absolute. The X coordinate always refers to the position left–right across the screen, the Y coordinate is the vertical position and the Z coordinate is the position in or out of the screen.

So, if you are looking at an object from the top, X is its width, Y its length and Z its height above the ground.

Figure 10.1   Looking down on the plan of a building

But if you look at it from the side, X is the width, but Y is the height and Z its length (or depth into the screen).

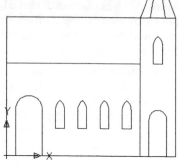

Figure 10.2 Looking at the same building from the side – X and Y are still in the same directions on the screen, but now refer to different dimensions on the object.

This could be confusing, as the same point will be at 20, 40, 60 or 20, 60, 40 or 60, 40, 20 depending upon which way you are looking at it. However, it does make drawing simpler as long as you are working in the same plane, because you only need to specify the X and Y coordinates.

An example will help to get your head round the key concepts. We are going to draw two squares – one above the other – by entering their coordinates. Notice that you give all X, Y and Z values for the first point, but only X and Y for the second. AutoCAD assumes that it is in the same plane.

1 Start a new drawing.

2 Click the rectangle tool. Enter the first corner as 0,0,0 and the second as 100,100.

3 Click the rectangle tool again. This time, enter the first corner as 0,0,50 and the second as 100,100.

4 Open the **View** menu, point to **3D Views** and select **SW Isometric**.

5 Try each of the 3D Views to see how the object looks.

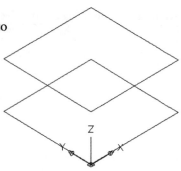

Figure 10.3 In isometric views, the bottom axes (X and Y in this example) are set at an angle of 30°, and parallel lines stay parallel – these are not perspective views.

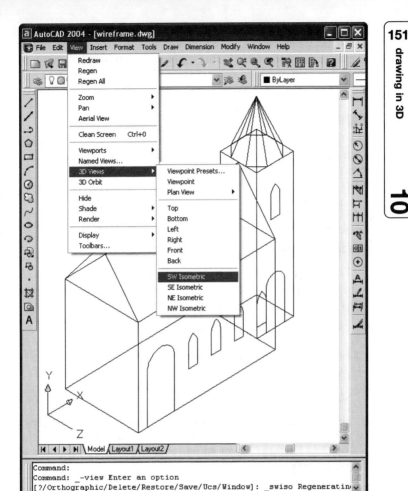

Figure 10.4 A wireframe drawing in an isometric view. The 3D View options also include flat-on views from the top, bottom, left, right, front and back. Notice how the direction of the X, Y, Z pointers is determined by the previous 'flat-on' view.

3D Polyline

The circle, arc, line and other drawing routines all behave in much the same way as the rectangle. You fix the first point in 3D space, then give only 2D coordinates for the later points. The object is then drawn flat-on to the screen at the depth set by the first Z coordinate.

The Draw menu includes a **3D Polyline** tool, which can be used to draw straight sided objects in 3D space. The standard Line tool can also be used to draw in 3D space, but it results in a series of linked lines while the 3D polyline is a single element.

Try this – it will draw an (almost) regular octahedron.

1 Start a new drawing, or erase the objects from the last trial.

2 Open the **Draw** menu and select **3D Polyline**.

3 Type the following sets of coordinates into the Command line:

50,50,-75	0,0,0	100,0,0
100,100,0	0,100,0	0,0,0
50,50,75	100,100,0	50,50,-75
100,0,0	50,50,75	0,100,0

4 Now view it through the 3D Views.

♦ Hmm! Because this is such a regular shape, the isometric views all look the same, as are the views from the sides or from the top and bottom. Never mind, there's another way to view 3D objects.

5 Open the **View** menu and select **3D Orbit**.

6 A green circle, with little circular handles at each quadrant, and a coloured X,Y,Z axes icon will appear. Drag on any part of the screen and the object will rotate in 3D space.

Controlling 3D orbits

The 3D Orbit routine can be a little tricky to control. Try to drag on a vertex – this gives a better correlation between the mouse movement and the movement of the object.

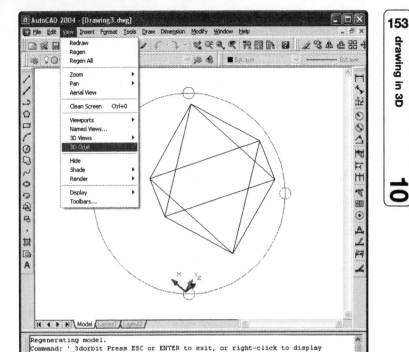

Figure 10.5 In 3D Orbit View you can rotate a drawing freely in any dimension.

Tips for drawing in 3D

Though you are using almost the same tools, drawing in 3D is different from drawing in 2D and you do need to change your approach.

- Never forget that there is a Z coordinate – and that it will refer different dimensions depending upon which way you are viewing model space.

- Apart from the Line, the standard drawing tools draw flat in the current plane, but you can set the Z depth when specifying the first coordinate.

- It takes a lot more coordinates to define a 3D shape! And compared with 2D work, the coordinates are more likely to be repeated. There will typically be three or more lines meeting at each vertex, and you may have to specify that vertex for each line.

♦ Drawing with the mouse is more difficult, because it is hard to control the cursor position in 3D space from a 2D mouse mat. It is not really feasible to pick coordinates – most will have to be entered through the Command line.

But...

♦ Object Snap works just as well in 3D space. Turn it on, then once a vertex is in place, you can join other lines to it quickly using the mouse. You need to be in an isometric view for this. Look at the spire on the church drawing in Figure 10.4 (page 151). To construct this, I first drew an 8-sided polygon on the top of the tower (by specifying the centre location and radius). I then switched to the 3D polyline tool, specified the position of the top of the spire, then drew the lines between the vertices of the polygon and the top of the spire using Object Snap.

♦ If you draw something in the wrong place, you can reposition it with the Move command – but specify the base point and the displacement point in the Command line, and check which way round the X,Y,Z pointers are facing before you do this!

♦ You can also reposition objects by editing their coordinates in the Properties palette.

Plotting 3D drawings

As a 3D drawing is as flat on the screen and on paper as a 2D drawing, it's no surprise that the same techniques are used when plotting. However, note these two points.

When you create a layout, the drawing will appear in the View mode that was current in model space. If required, you can change to a different mode now – simply open the View menu and pick a 3D View option.

There is a simple way of creating a plan-and-elevation plot. At the Define Viewports step of the Layout Wizard there is an option **Std. 3D Engineering Views**. Choose this to get a top, side, end and isometric view on a single plot.

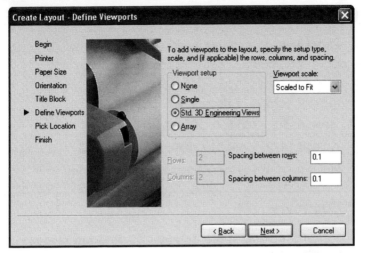

Figure 10.6 The Std. 3D Engineering View is the simplest way to get multiple plots of a 3D drawing.

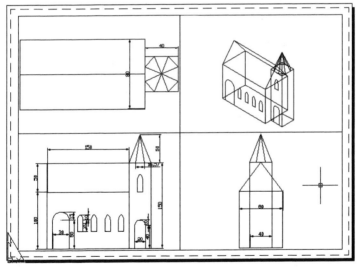

Figure 10.7 In this layout, dimensions have been added to the standard 3D engineering view. If required, you can change any or all of the views – click into the view to select then pick a new mode from the View menu.

Exercises

1 Either draw a wireframe model of a house of your choice, or of the dog kennel. The kennel's dimensions are shown in the screenshot on page 137. You can work out most of the coordinates from that. If the bottom front left corner is at 0, 0, 0 then the corners of the roof are:

50,450,-50; -300,850,-50; -650,450,-50;

50,450,1050; -300,850,1050; -650,450,1050.

2 Plot your drawing using Engineering view layout.

Summary

- AutoCAD has three different 3D drawing modes: wireframe, surface and solid.

- The X,Y,Z coordinate system is screen-based – not absolute.

- The View menu includes a set of 3D view options.

- Lines, rectangles and circles can be drawn in 3D, but only in the same plane as the screen.

- With 3D polylines you can construct objects anywhere in 3D space.

- The Std. 3D Engineering View is the simplest way to get multiple plots of a 3D drawing.

3D solids

In this chapter you will learn:

- how to define and use 3D solids
- how to combine solids to create new shapes
- about the Shade options
- how to render an image

Defining solids

AutoCAD has a comprehensive system for drawing solids. It would take a whole book to describe it fully – there is only room here to give an introduction to its possibilities. We will look at how basic shapes can be defined, then combined to create new shapes, and also explore ways of viewing 3D models. If you follow the examples given here, you will finish up with a solid model of the church that you saw as a wireframe in Chapter 10. (I like the irony of modelling a 13th century building in 21st century software.)

When working with solids, you should have the **Solids** toolbar open. We will only be using the five tools labelled here. Explore the others later when you have an hour or two to spare.

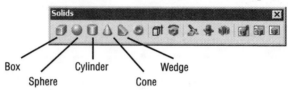

Box   Cylinder   Wedge
     Sphere   Cone

Sphere

We will start with the sphere, because it gives a good illustration of the display options for solids. The tool draws a perfect sphere around a point.

To draw a sphere:

1 Click the **Sphere** tool on the **Solids** toolbar.

2 Switch to a suitable view – Front view is good when starting on a model.

3 Enter the coordinates of the central point.

4 Enter the radius of the sphere.

◆ You should see a circle with an inner circle and crossing diameters. In a flat-on view it doesn't look much like a sphere.

5 Open the **View** menu, point to **3D Views** and select an isometric view.

◆ You should now see an outline of the sphere, drawn from five interlinked circles. This is the standard 3D wireframe display.

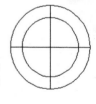

We can get a better-looking sphere by changing the View option. Open the **View** menu and select **Hide**.

♦ This removes the 'hidden' lines – the ones at the back of the model, and adds more lines to emphasize curves. When you change the view, the display will revert to the full wireframe. (See *The Shade options* on page 167 for more on display modes.)

There are no spheres in our model, so you might want to remove the test sphere – select it and press [**Delete**].

Box

To define a box, you first give the position of one corner. You can then specify its size in three different ways:

by giving the X,Y,Z position of the opposite corner;

by giving the length (X), width (Y) and height (Z);

by specifying 'cube' and giving the length of a side.

And remember that the direction of the X,Y,Z axes depend upon the view you are in.

To create a box:

1 Click the **Box** tool on the Solids toolbar.

2 Switch to **Front** view.

3 Enter the position of a corner (usually the bottom left front), e.g. 0,0,0.

4 Specify the opposite corner, e.g. 150,80,100 – this produces a box 150 long by 80 wide and 100 high.

5 Open the **View** menu, point to **3D Views** and select an isometric view.

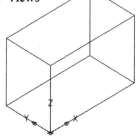

♦ If you want to make the church, you will need a second box for the tower. This should start at 150,20,0 and should be 40 long, 40 wide and 150 high.

Cone

A cone is defined by the position of the centre of its base, the radius of the base and the height of the cone. It will be drawn with the base in the same plane as the screen – so make sure that you are in a suitable view when you start.

1 Click the **Cone** tool on the Solids toolbar.

2 Switch to the appropriate view – Top in our example.

3 Enter the position of the centre of the base – to draw one at the top of our tower you should enter 170,40,150.

4 Enter the radius, e.g. 20.

5 Enter the height, e.g. 50.

6 Switch to an isometric view so that you can see how it looks.

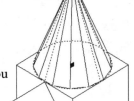

Wedge

Wedges can be awkward! They are drawn with the base in the same plane as the screen and sloping down across the screen (the highest end will be over the start position).

They can be defined in several ways. The simplest is probably to give the opposite corner of the base, and then the height. But however you define a wedge, it is still very easy to create one that slopes the wrong way, or that faces the wrong way. If it slopes the wrong way, delete it and start again. If it faces the wrong way, it can easily be turned round – as you will see if you work through the next example. We are trying to create a roof for the main part of the church model.

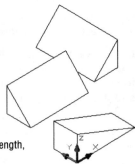

Figure 11.1 These wedges all have the same length, width and height but are quite different shapes.

To make a wedge:

1 Pick a view where the base of the wedge will be flat on to the screen – Top in our example.

2 Click the **Wedge** tool on the Solids toolbar.

3 Enter the coordinates of a corner at the high end of the wedge – 0,40,100 for our example.

4 Enter the coordinates of the opposite corner of the base – e.g. 40,190,100. (This creates a wedge 40 wide by 150 long.)

5 Enter the height – for our roof this should be 50.

6 Switch to the **SW Isometric** view.

♦ You should have a wedge of the right shape for (half) the roof, but in the wrong place. No problem! This can be easily rotated into place.

To rotate a solid:

1 Click on the solid to select it.

2 Make sure that **Object Snap** and **Polar** are turned on.

3 Click the **Rotate** tool on the Modify toolbar.

4 Click on the corner of the solid at 0,40,100.

5 Using the rotate guideline, swing the wedge through 270° to bring it into the right place.

♦ Create the other half of the roof by constructing a wedge of the same shape at 150,40,100 and rotating it through 90°.

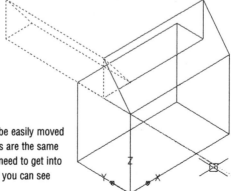

Figure 11.2 Shapes can be easily moved and rotated. The techniques are the same as for 2D objects, but you need to get into a suitable view first so that you can see what you are doing.

Cylinder

The last solid we will be using in our model is the cylinder, and we need this to create the arches above the doors and windows.

Like the solids, a cylinder is drawn with its base in the same plane as the screen. As the cylinders in this model will come out from the front wall, we need to view our drawing from the front. This example is the first stage in constructing the main door in our church model.

To create a cylinder:

1 Switch to a suitable view, **Front** in this case.

2 Enter the coordinates of the centre point, e.g. 25,50,-5.

3 Enter the radius, e.g. 15.

4 Enter the height – 10 for this example.

To complete the doorway, we need a box of the same width as the cylinder to fill the space down to the ground. Construct a box 30 wide by 50 high by 10 deep. (Start from 10,0,-5.)

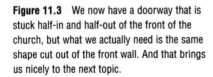

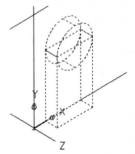

Figure 11.3 We now have a doorway that is stuck half-in and half-out of the front of the church, but what we actually need is the same shape cut out of the front wall. And that brings us nicely to the next topic.

Redefining solids

You cannot adjust the corners of solids in the same way as 2D objects. If you want to adjust the shape of a solid, you can do it by moving its surfaces (use the Move command on the Solids Editing toolbar). In practice, you may well find it simpler and quicker to delete a mis-shaped solid and create a new one.

Combining solids

If two or more solids touch or overlap, they can be combined to create a single new shape. There are three tools:

• **Union** joins the solids into one, absorbing any overlaps.

• **Subtract** removes the overlapping volume, creating a cavity. (The rest of the subtracted solid is also removed completely.)

• **Intersect** removes everything except the overlap.

We will use all three in our model. You will find the tools on the **Solids Editing** toolbar. Turn it on now if it is not visible.

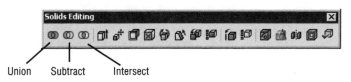

Union   Subtract   Intersect

Union

This is probably the simplest of the tools. Use it to join the two parts of the doorway.

To join solids:

1 Click the **Union** tool on the Solids Editing toolbar.

2 Hold down [**Shift**] and click on the solids to be joined – they should all be shown in dotted lines. If you select a solid by mistake, click on it again to deselect it.

3 Right-click to create the union.

• Join the two roof wedges in the same way.

Figure 11.4 The doorway solid after the union operation. We can now subtract it from the main block to create an opening.

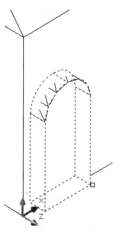

Subtract

To subtract one solid from another:

1 Check that the solids are intersecting in the right way.

2 Click the **Subtract** tool.

3 Click to select the solid from which you want to subtract the overlap (the main body of the church, in our example). If there are several solids, hold **[Shift]** while you click. Right-click when you have done to move on to the next part of the operation.

4 Select the solid(s) to be subtracted (the doorway), and right-click when you have done.

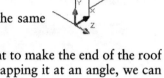

♦ You should now have a hole the same shape as the overlap.

Let's take a second example. I want to make the end of the roof slope. If we create a big box overlapping it at an angle, we can use the subtract tool to cut off the end.

1 Go to **Front** view.

2 Construct a box, starting at 0,100,0 (i.e. the bottom corner of the roof), with the opposite corner at -80,180,-80.

This is bigger than is needed, but it doesn't matter.

3 Rotate the box around its start point, so that it overlaps the roof by 15° or more.

4 Click on the **Subtract** tool.

5 Select the roof as the base from which to subtract.

6 Select the block as the solid to subtract.

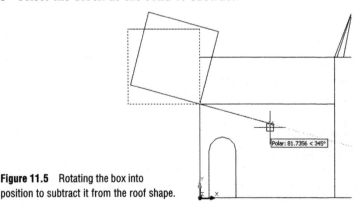

Figure 11.5 Rotating the box into position to subtract it from the roof shape.

Intersect

I want a pointed arch on the windows of the church model – and I know I'm mixing Norman and early Perpendicular architectural styles, but this is only an example! On a 2D drawing, this could be created with two interlocking arcs. In 3D, we can produce the shape by intersecting two cylinders. Try this.

1 Go to **Front** view.

2 Construct a cylinder with the centre at 55,50,0, radius 10, height 10.

♦ It should appear on the church wall to the right of the doorway.

3 Create a second cylinder with the centre at 65,50,0, radius 10, height 10.

♦ The two should overlap as shown here – this is seen in SW isometric view.

4 Click the **Intersect** tool on the Solids Editing toolbar.

5 Hold down [**Shift**] and select the two cylinders.

6 Right-click to complete the operation.

This doesn't look much like an arched window!

1 Add a box to complete the shape. It should be 10 wide, 20 high and 10 deep, starting at 55,30, 0 (working in **Front** view).

2 Join the two shapes together with the **Union** tool.

3 The 'window' is on the surface of the wall. It needs to be pushed back into it. No problem!

4 Select the window shape.

5 Click the **Move** tool on the Modify toolbar.

6 Enter 55,30,0 as the base point.

7 Enter 55,30,-5 as the second point.

♦ Yes, we could have sunk the cylinders and the box into the wall when we created them, but then you wouldn't have got to try out the **Move** command!

Copying solids

There are no special tricks here – it is almost identical to copying in 2D. You will find it helps to work in the view which brings the solids into the same plane as the screen so that coordinates are easier to work with. You may also find it helps to have Object Snap turned on. You will need to give the coordinates of a base point, and if you snap to a corner they will be displayed in the Status bar.

Copy the window shape three times along the front of the church, leaving a gap of 15 between each pair. If you use its bottom left corner as the base point, the copy points should be 80,10,-5 then 105,10,-5 and 130,10,-5.

You can now subtract the window shapes from the main block.

You should have a model which looks something like this.

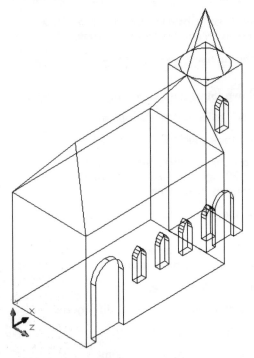

Figure 11.6 The model as a 3D wireframe. I have added a window and door to the tower – you may like to do the same.

The Shade options

If you look on the **View** menu you will find a **Shade** entry which leads to a submenu. This has several display options, including:

* **3D wireframe** is the default. This shows only the edges of the surfaces and the main curves of arcs and cylinders.

* **Hidden** removes the lines that would be hidden if the front surfaces were solid, giving a more realistic view of the model. The **View > Hide** option has the same effect, but reverts to wireframe when the model is redrawn.

* **Flat shaded** fills the surfaces with flat colour. Curves are displayed as a series of flat planes.

* **Gourand shaded** produces smoother curves.

* Both of the shaded options have **Edges On** variants.

In the default layer colour of black, you can scarcely see the differences between these shade options. Either change the colour of the whole model by changing the Layer definition, or recolour one solid by selecting it, opening its Properties panel and picking a new colour.

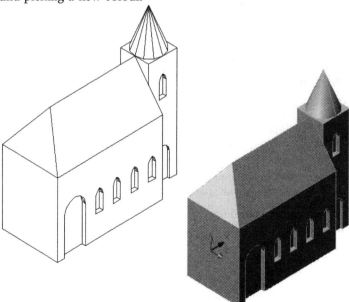

Figure 11.7 The model in Hidden and Gourand shaded modes.

The order of the options on the Shade menu is significant. Going down the list, each successive mode requires more computing power and so takes longer to draw. On a small model, you will not notice the difference, but it soon becomes appreciable – have a look at the 3D samples supplied with AutoCAD.

As a general rule, stay in 3D wireframe mode while building the model, switching into Hidden if you need a clearer overview, and only use Shaded modes when you are preparing the final output. And for final output, you might want to use rendering. Read on!

Rendering

For the most realistic image, you should *render* the model, giving textures to the surface, placing lights around it and even adding a background. The tools can be found on the **View > Render** submenu or on the Render toolbar. The key ones are labelled here.

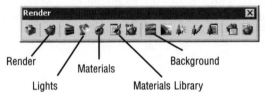

Materials

These give textures and colours to surfaces. AutoCAD supplies a range of materials effects, including plastic, glass, stone and wood and you can use your own bitmap images. The materials are stored in a library, and you must start there. The first job is to select the materials that you want to use in the drawing, so that their definitions can be incorporated into the files. The next job is to attach the materials to solids.

To select your materials:

1 Click the **Materials Library** button or select **View > Render > Materials Library...**

2 Scroll through the list of materials on the right of the box.

3 Click **Preview** to see what a material looks like – you can select Cube and Sphere from the drop-down list below it.

4 If you want to be able to use the material, click **Import** to copy it into the **Current Drawing** list.

5 When you have all the materials you need, click **OK**.

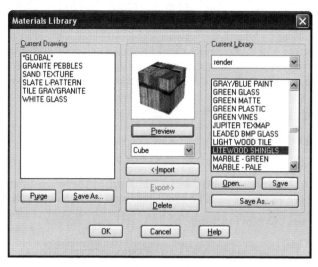

To apply a material to a solid:

1 Click the **Materials** button or use **View > Render > Materials...**

2 Select a material from the list – click **Preview** if you want to check its appearance.

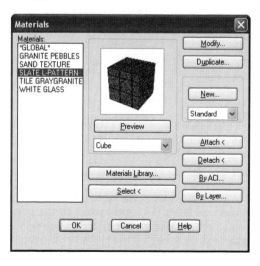

3 Click **Attach**. The dialog box will disappear. Select the solids which are to have this surface effect, then right-click to end the selection and restore the dialog box.

4 Repeat from step 2 to attach other materials to other objects.

5 Click **OK** when you have done.

The image will look exactly the same as it did before you started! All you have done so far is set things up for rendering. The effects are only made visible when you run the rendering routine.

Render

To render a scene:

1 Click the **Render** button or use **View > Render > Render...**

2 The **Render** dialog box will open. Turn on the **Smooth Shade**, **Apply Materials** and **Shadows** options in the lower left.

3 Leave the other options for now and click **Render**.

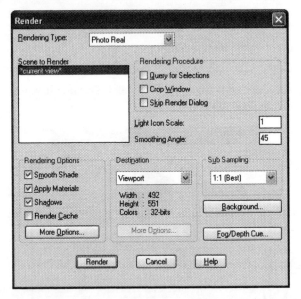

- AutoCAD will think for a moment then redraw the model with textured surfaces. As soon as you zoom, pan or change the view, the model will revert to its previous, simpler, display mode.

Lights

Lights help to set the scene. You can control the overall colour
and brightness through the Ambient Light options, and set up
additional light sources. Experimentation and close observation
are needed here to work out how best to light a scene.

To control the Ambient Light:

1 Click the **Lights** button or use **View > Render > Light...**

2 Use the **Intensity** slider to set the overall brightness.

3 Use the **Red, Green, Blue** sliders to adjust the colour, or click
Select Color... and pick from the palette.

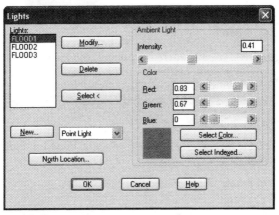

To add extra lights:

4 Click **New...**

5 At the **New Spotlight** dialog box, define the colour and intensity of the light.

6 Click the **Modify** button to set the position – you can adjust
this later if necessary.

7 Click **OK** to return to the Lights dialog box, and click **OK**
there when you have finished setting up the lights.

8 If you look closely, you will find the spotlights
in model space. They can be moved just like any
other object.

9 Render the image again to see the effect of your lights.

Figure 11.8 The model after adding materials and lights.

Background

You can give your rendered model a coloured or picture background. The colour can be solid, or a gradient effect, shading across three colours. The picture can be any bitmap image, and can be stretched or 'tiled' to fill the window. We'll use an image.

To set a background:

1 Click the **Background** button or select **View > Render > Background...**

2 Select **Image** for the type of background.

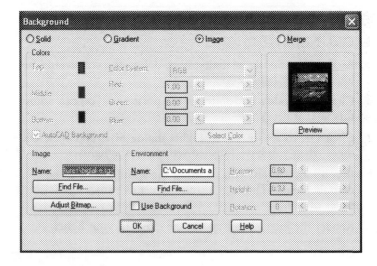

3 In the **Image** area, click **Find File...** and locate the picture file. AutoCAD will offer you its selection of .tga background and texture files, or you can look elsewhere in your system – change the type of file if you are looking for .bmp, .gif or other types.

4 Click **Preview** to get an idea of how the image will look.

5 Click **OK** to end.

6 Use **Render** to see the model on its background.

♦ If the background is a landscape, you may be able to get your model to fit into it by adjusting its position, angle and zoom level. Unfortunately, every time you adjust the display it will revert to its simpler Shade mode.

Figure 11.9 The finished rendered model on its background. This has been just a quick example to show what is possible – I'm sure that you could do better.

Exercises

1 Start a new drawing and make sure that you are in Top view.

Create a box with the coordinates 0,0,0 and 400,300,200.

Create a cylinder centred at 200,150,0 with a radius of 60 and a height of 200.

Create a second box with the coordinates 150,100,400 and 250,200,600.

Switch to an isometric view then subtract the cylinder from the first box.

Change to a flat or Gourand shaded display mode.

You should now have a square peg and a round hole!

2 Experiment with these techniques to produce your own 3D models. When you have mastered them, explore the Extrude and Rotate tools – they can turn flat surfaces into 3D solids, allowing you to create more complex objects.

Summary

- AutoCAD has a comprehensive system for drawing solids.

- You can use the tools to create a box, sphere, cylinder, cone, wedge or torus.

- Objects are usually created flat-on to the plane of the screen.

- Solids can be modified in the same way as 2D objects, using the tools on the Modify toolbar.

- Where solids overlap, they can be merged in different ways by the Union, Subtract and Intersect tools.

- You can display a model as a wireframe, or with hidden lines removed, or shaded using the Shade options.

- Rendering produces a more realistic image. The model can be enhanced in various ways, including adding textures to surfaces, setting up lights and giving it a background.

taking it further

This book should have helped to get you started with AutoCAD, but it won't have made you an expert – there's a lot more to learn before you can claim that label!

The Help system in AutoCAD is very thorough – possibly too thorough. There is so much information that it can take a while to filter the many possible topics to find the one that answers your question. Persevere. The more familiar that you are with AutoCAD, and with its Help system, the easier it becomes to get the Help that you need.

There is lots of help and other resources available online. The Online Resources entry in the Help menu leads to links to the product support, training and customization at Autodesk's web site (www.autodesk.com), and to the Autodesk User Group's site (www.augi.com). You can also get help from and share your ideas with other users through the 30 or so newsgroups devoted to aspects of AutoCAD – look up 'autocad' in the newsgroup subscription routine of your mail and news reader.

If you want recognition of your AutoCAD skills, why not try for a certificate or diploma. In the UK, City & Guilds offers qualifications at several levels, as do other organizations elsewhere. A search for 'AutoCAD' and 'examination' at Google should lead you to your local testing authority.

But the most important thing that you can do to take your AutoCAD expertise further is to experiment and explore. There are so many tools and routines to play with – enjoy them!

index

3D Engineering Views **154**
3D modes **149**
3D orbits **152**
3D Polyline **152**

Aligned dimension **95**
Angular dimension **96**
Architectural units **134**
Arcs **33**
Array **52**
Auto-hide **76**
AutoCAD options **28**
AutoCAD window **2**
Axes, and the screen **150**

Background **172**
Baseline dimension **98**
Blocks
  editing **121**
  inserting **120**, **124**
  making **118**
Box **159**
Break **59**
ByBlock **67**
ByLayer **67**

Cartesian coordinates **16**
Chamfer **27**, **61**
Circles **30**
Circumscribed polygon **32**
Colour, in layers **115**
Colour setting **71**
Command Line window **3**

Cone **160**
Construction lines **31**
Continuation lines **35**
Coordinates
  entering **10**
  relative **16**
  specifying **16**
Copy **49**
  solids **166**
Cylinder **162**

Decimal units **134**
DesignCenter **123**
DesignCenter Online **126**
Diameter dimension **95**
Dimension style **102**
Dimensions **93**
Drafting Settings **14**
Draw menu **26**
Draw toolbar **26**
Drawing in 3D **153**
Drawing limits **9**
Drawing units **8**, **134**
Drawings, inserting **120**

Elevation **28**, **131**
Ellipse arcs **37**
Ellipses **36**
Engineering units **134**
Erase **48**
Explode **63**
Extend **58**

Feet and inches **17**
Fillet **28**, **62**
Flat shaded **167**
Freezing **111**

Gourand shaded **167**
Gradient fills **85**
Grid **13**

Hatch Edit **84**
Hatches
  and layers **84**
  as objects **83**
  defining **80**
Hidden line removal **167**

Inscribed polygon **32**
Intersect **165**

Layer Properties Manager **113**
Layers **110**
  creating **113**
Layers toolbar **111**
Layout Wizard **144**
Layouts **137**
Leaders **100**
Lights **171**
Line colour **71**
Linear dimension **94**
Lines **17**
Linetype **69**
  in layers **115**
Lineweight **67**
  in layers **115**

Materials **168**
Materials Library **168**
Mirror **50**
Model space **7**, **133**
  from a layout **139**
Modify toolbar **48**
Mouse
  buttons **5**
  drawing **12**
  wheel **7**
Move **55**
  solids **165**

Multiline text **92**

Object snap **14**
Objects, editing **42**
Offset **52**
Opening files **21**
Options, setting **28**
Ordinate dimension **97**
Orthographic projection **131**

Paper output **133**
Paper sizes **134**
Paper space **7**
Pick **12**
Plan **131**
Plotters **142**
Plotting 3D drawings **154**
Point and type **29**
Points **37**
Polar coordinates **16**
Polar tracking **13**, **50**
Polygons **32**
Polylines **38**
Preview **143**
Properties palette **73**
Properties toolbar **67**

Quick dimension **96**

Radius dimension **95**
Rectangles **26**
Rendering **168**
Rotate **55**
  solids **161**

Saving files **19**
Scales **56**, **133**
  and units **125**
  problems **142**
  standard **134**
Selecting objects **42**
Setting up **136**
Shade options **167**
Single line text **90**
Sketches **130**
Snap **13**
Solid models **149**

Solids
  combining **163**
  copying **166**
  defining **158**
  moving **165**
  redefining **162**
  rotating **161**
Sphere **158**
Splines **35**
Stretch **57**
Subtract **163**
Surface drawings **149**

Text
  dimensions **104**
  multiline **92**
  single line **90**
  size **92**
Thaw **111**
Thickness, in rectangles **28**
Tolerance **100**
Toolbars **2**
  Dimension **93**
  Draw **26**

Layers **111**
Modify **48**
Properties **67**
Refedit **122**
Render **168**
Solids **158**
Solids Editing **163**
Trim **58**

Union **163**
Units of measurement, AutoCAD **8**

Vertex **154**
  changing in Properties palette **75**
View options **151**
Viewports **140**

Wedge **160**
Wheel mouse **7**
Wireframe drawings **149**

Z coordinate **149**
Zoom **11**

teach
yourself

html: publishing on the www
mac bride

- Are you an Internet user?
- Do you want to move from browsing to publishing?
- Do you want to explore the possibilities of HTML?

HTML: Publishing on the WWW takes the mystery out of the technical issues and jargon of web site building. It covers the whole of HTML, from the very basics through to style sheets, clearly explained and with worked examples throughout. With this book you can learn enough to create a colourful, illustrated web page in just a few hours, or to put together a full-featured, interactive, interlinked web site in a few days.

Mac Bride is a successful computer author who brings over 20 years of teaching experience to his writing.

| teach yourself | **Photoshop**
christopher lumgair |

- Do you need a basic introduction to Photoshop?
- Do you want help with creating images or web pages?
- Do you need to brush up your Photoshop skills?

Photoshop introduces you to the essentials of this industry-standard tool. The book guides you through Photoshop's image-editing, photo-retouching and web-enabling features in easy-to-follow stages, concentrating on those techniques and processes which will enable you to create sophisticated-looking images and feature-rich web pages with the minimum of effort.

Christopher Lumgair has a BA in Graphic Design and has spent several years working in both magazine and book publishing. He now runs his own successful digital publishing consultancy.

teach yourself

Java
chris wright

- Do you want to program confidently in Java?
- Do you need to enhance your web site?
- Do you want to build interactive pages?

Java is a clear guide to programming in Java 2, the language which powers the Internet. It teaches the core skills necessary to produce coherent, maintainable code to enhance web sites and build interactive pages, and covers graphics, communications, GUI design and object orientation and threads.

Chris Wright is a specialist in distributed object oriented systems and delivers training and consultancy across Europe and the UK.